*E*ndorsem
W
DE

This book goes beyond just good thoughts and ideas but carry's the very heart of God. These bite-sized truths are transferable to whatever situation you are in and are genuine gems that will inspire and enrich you and your team. Cannot recommend highly enough.

Simon Triffitt, Worship Pastor,
Life Church, Folkestone, UK

I have known Matt Lockwood for quite a number of years and I have to say, *he is the real deal.* His insatiable passion for Jesus, his love for the local church and love for 'the team' radiate from these writings. I know you will be encouraged and strengthened as you read these pages. This book is an insight into how you can build both a relevant and practical team and also a spiritually deep and alive team. It's a challenge to remain consistent in doing both. Family Church is to be commended for its flourishing culture. Matt is faithfully committed to outworking 'the vision' alongside his Pastors, leaders and team. He is an asset to God's great church. Matt, I pray continued blessing on all that you and the team are reaching for in these days!

Mark Stevens, Worship Leader and Pastor,
Alive Church Harrogate, UK

Matt's anointing in worship is evident when he is on the platform with a guitar, when he is teaching behind the pulpit and even now when he has a pen in his hand. With his short deliberate chapters just like the dots and dashes in Morse Code he communicates important information and revelation into a worshipper's heart. This book will be our Worship Team's manual and I recommend it for yours also. A hearty "Well done!", Matt.

Danny Thornton, Senior Pastor,
River of Life Family Church, Syracuse, USA

The absolute throb of this insightful book by Matt is purely this: honesty in worship, selfless and servant-hearted worship. I highly and vigorously commend this gritty work as an invaluable resource. It's not just for worship teams, but for the church as a whole, genuinely and transparently engaging with the heart of the individual, and highlighting the power of 'one sound' in corporate worship.

Michael Dalton, Worship Leader,
Riversong Music, Australia

Worship ministry is a high calling, a pressured ministry and one that is highly visible to people in your church. Matt Lockwood is an outstanding Team Leader, Worship Leader, Songwriter and family man. He has an innate ability to listen to others and to God and has always been keen to ask questions and gain new perspectives on life, ministry and worship. *Worship Devotions* is a comprehensive guide to building a worship team, creating a culture of worship in the local church and provides biblical and practical principles and insights for those involved in worship ministry and for worshippers within the Church at large. Everyone needs to read this outstanding book and apply the principles and ideas outlined in its pages to their own ministry.

David Reidy, Worship Pastor, Teacher and Lecturer,
Hillsong Church, Sydney, Australia

A fantastic collection of devotionals that really captures the heart, values and vision of a great worship team! A 'must-read' for any worship team committed to serving the church and the Kingdom of God in a greater way.

Stephanie Martin-Papp, Worship Pastor,
Life Church Poole, UK

Worship of God is not a skill that can be learned, it is an expression from a heart that knows it has been made alive through the perfect work of Jesus Christ. God never teaches us to how worship, He simply is the only One worthy of it. We first met Matt in 1992 when we were pastoring a young church and raising our family. Worship was natural to Matt – it flowed from his heart with ease and authenticity, and with a contagious force that we and the church instantly came to appreciate. His genuine love for Jesus expressed through worship impacted the church family greatly. As you read this book don't search for tips on how to lead worship but let your heart be impacted with the love, devotion and appreciation for God that truly is at the core of genuine worship.

John & Jo Harris, Senior Pastors,
The Nations International Church, Suwon, South Korea

This book contains such nuggets of wisdom and inspiration. Knowing Matt and the Family Church team I know this is also backed up by hearts on fire for God and a passion for God and His glory. This is a must have for any worship pastor or worship team. I know that you'll get as much out of it as I already have!

Gareth Matthews, Worship Pastor and Assistant Leader,
King's Church, Portsmouth, UK

WORSHIP
DEVOTIONS

WORSHIP DEVOTIONS

Sowing vision one thought at a time

MATT LOCKWOOD

This edition published in 2017 by Great Big Life Publishing
Empower Centre, 83-87 Kingston Road, Portsmouth, PO2 7DX, UK.

British Library Cataloguing in Publication Data. A catalogue record for this book
is available from the British Library

ISBN-13: 978-0-9957925-2-4
ISBN-10: 0995792526
eBook ISBN: 978-0-9957925-3-1

CONTENTS

FOREWORD

When I first floated the idea of building a strong church in Portsmouth with my closest friend Wayne, back in the late 90's, there were three things we both agreed needed to be the foundation of this new church – preaching the undiluted Word of God, passionate and authentic worship, and a dynamic, life-affirming kids work. In the many years since starting Family Church, those three 'foundation stones' have continued to undergird our growth, discipleship and outreach. We are now a multi-site, multi-congregation church with weekly salvations, increasing connect groups, community programs that reach out to local children, the homeless, vulnerable women and their families, and numerous missions trips throughout the year headed out across the globe. As the senior pastor of a growing, missional church, I know that having a healthy and authentic corporate worship life has been vital to our church.

I first met Matt over twenty years ago. He had already developed as a passionate and anointed worship leader, but over the years I have watched him grow into a strong team leader, able to bring clear vision and direction to our whole worship team, across the growing number of congregations. As Family Church, and my own speaking ministry with it, has grown in number and influence, Matt's leadership has grown to not only manage the day-to-day running of a large team of creative individuals spread out over a large geographical area, but to remain ahead, seeing what God is taking the church into and prophetically speak it into the worship team so that they in turn can lead the church. His own influence as a worship team pastor and leader has grown like ivy beyond the reach of his own church 'garden' into the growing sphere of ministry friends that have connected with Family Church over the years.

What follows in this collection is the unveiling of Matt's heart for worship teams and congregations: a desire to see musicians and singers understand the depth and breadth of their calling and ministry, the responsibility they carry and the opportunity they have to make incredible impact for God's kingdom; and a passion to see the church unite in corporate worship, to throw off flakey, wishy-washy, religious, and shallow worship experience and pursue an encounter with God that will radically change the communities in which we live.

Prepare to be challenged, prepare to get offended, prepare to to have your heart sliced up in front of you and put back together by the wisdom of the Holy Spirit and the unfailing truth of God's Word. But most of all, prepare to grow and find greater liberty and boldness as you lead your teams, as you lead your congregations and as you lead yourself in worship.

I highly commend Matt to you – not just as a worship leader but as a devoted worshipper – and this book as the thoughts of a man who desires to give God pure worship and nothing else. I know that as you read it you won't be able to put it down, and a fresh desire will grow within you to be the worshipper Jesus has called you to be. Go with it, living to worship Him in Spirit and in truth.

Andy Elmes
Senior Pastor, Family Church

INTRODUCTION

This book is a collection of thoughts and messages that were written for the weekly team emails that go out to the congregational worship teams of Family Church, a multi-national church with (currently, as of January 2017) eight congregations across the South Coast of England, and two in the Philippines, between 2012 and 2016.

Many of these devotionals refer to church events, or messages from the Family Church pastors (I've added explanatory footnotes for clarification). The purpose of these messages was to carry some nugget of our culture and vision each week, along with details of song lists and line-ups for the coming weekend.

This devotional is not just aimed at worship leaders, pastors and worship team members, but anyone with a heart and desire to live a life of worship, honouring Jesus Christ in every area, season and opportunity that He leads us into.

I hope and pray that these thoughts inspire and challenge you, whether you are leading a worship team, a member of a worship team, or just interested in it all. We are all on a journey, and we all have so much to learn.

I would love to hear back from you, so get in touch with me through the social network links below.

Thanks,

Matt Lockwood

Links

Matt Lockwood
🐦 @mattlockwood
📷 @mattjlockwood73
f facebook.com/worshipteam101
🖵 worshipteam101.com

Family Church Worship Team
🐦 @FC_Worship
📷 @familychurchcreative
f facebook.com/familychurchworshipteam
🖵 family.church/creative

Family Church
🐦 @_familychurch
📷 @thisisfamilychurch
f facebook.com/thisisfamilychurch
🖵 family.church

DEDICATION

To Ali, Zach, Caleb and Matilda –
this adventure gets more interesting and exciting every
day, and I'm so thankful to have you to share it with;

and

to the Family Church Worship Team –
thank you for giving me the privilege of leading you,
let's never forget who we carry, what we carry, and why.

Devotions

uilt on vision

#vision #heart

Team isn't built around certain people but on vision and principles that remain no matter who is involved.

That vision and those principles need to be grounded in our hearts, not just thoughts we consider good or reasonable. It's when something is in our hearts that it becomes a part of who we are.

Always, what we do is built on the vision to 'carry God's people into His presence, and carry God's presence to His people, through character and creativity'.

Get the vision

Vision is vital for the health and growth of a team. It's never enough to just turn up and do the job, we must know and see why we do it for what we do to be more effective, for it to be more than entertainment, for it to have spiritual impact on the lives of everyone that comes to our church (and beyond).

The vision of our team is to carry God's presence to His people, and to carry God's people into His presence, through our character and our creativity. I want to encourage all of you to not just read the words and gloss over them, but to take some time to mull them over, and to ask God what they mean to you, and how you can walk them out.

I've never wanted to build a team where I make certain rules that we all adhere to because there's no passion or love in following rules. But when we each grab hold of the vision and see how God wants each of us to live it out, then the little things fall into place, the reason behind our style and way of doing things make sense, the things you're asked to do stop being chores and become a delight.

But more than that, you understand God's purpose for your life, and your relationship with Him grows stronger, and that's what's most important – because at the end of the day God isn't after our talents or the things we do, or the time we give; He's after us, just us.

The heartbeat of our team

#selfless #heartbeat #Elisha #musicianship

I was reminded this weekend, after the Dambusters prayer meeting, of a passage in 2 Kings where the prophet Elisha calls for a musician to help him get an answer from God for a massive situation he'd been handed.

> *"But now bring me a musician." Then it happened, when the musician played, that the hand of the Lord came upon him.*
> **2 Kings 3:15**

The king of Israel, with the kings of Judah and Edom, were heading to Moab to deal with their king, but on the way they'd run out of water. They were heading into a massive fight without the basic resources, their armies and horses were tired and thirsty, they'd committed themselves to this course and they could see no way of getting success.

Elisha needs to hear God's word on this situation – otherwise he could have the death of his own king, and two others, on his hands. On this occasion he chooses to have a musician play while he gets before

God and seeks for the breakthrough they all need.

The answer comes, and the victory is gained for the king of Israel – an impossible situation turned completely around.

Nothing is given about the musician that played for Elisha. We don't know who he or she was; we don't know what they played, or how good they were. They just served for the moment. They created for Elisha an atmosphere and pathway where he could get beyond the pressure from the three national leaders he was facing, to being able to hear God's voice clearly. There's no indication of any acknowledgement, thanks or payment for the musician afterwards; just the mention of their selfless act of service.

That selfless offering is worship itself. That's the heartbeat of our team.

Why do we have band nights?

PART 1

#bandnight #team #family #relationship

Every church does it differently – maybe not always the most effectively, but differently!

Having a regular night for the band may seem an obvious thing to do, but actually the reasons for doing so go beyond rehearsing for the coming weekend. Here are a few reasons why we do it:

1. Band nights are for family

One of the founding purposes of Family Church is to be a living expression of God's family, one that isn't defined by surname or natural birth, but by the Word of God that says that we are all His sons and daughters, brought into His family through Jesus' blood shed on the cross, removing us from darkness into His light and having His nature within us.

The worship team is just a small part of that family expressed in Family Church. The team is one of many opportunities we have to serve our family, and within this team we continue to express that family.

Family is built on relationship, not jobs, roles or positions. The strength of what we do, how we serve, is built on our relationships with each other – relationships that come because of being family, not because of being able to play or sing. What we do is built on love, not on skill or talent.

Our band nights give time for our relationships to develop and strengthen. We need to come each night with an attitude to serve, honour, respect and encourage. Difficulties and disagreements need to be worked through from a perspective of love and united purpose.

Selfish ambition, personal agendas, gripes, jealousy, insecurity – these things will always destroy family, in any situation, and come from not opening and surrendering to family relationships. There is always strength, love, acceptance and protection in family, and our team should reflect that. That's more important than what we play or sing, because our relationships will outlast our time in the worship team.

Why do we have band nights?

PART 2

#vision #growth #leadership

2. Band nights are for vision

A people without vision will perish (Proverbs 29:18). You need to know why you're doing something or you'll lose motivation and passion, and end up drifting along or feeling chained and controlled.

Habakkuk 2:2 says, "Write the vision and make it plain . . . that he may run who reads it". Vision brings inspiration, focus and direction. It brings passion and energy.

One of the reasons why we ask everyone in the team to come every week is that keeping vision before us as a team is vital if we're all to remain going in the same direction, and the same direction as the team leaders. It's easy in the week-in-week-out, regular things of life to just do what we do each week and slowly forget why we do them. Coming to band night and hearing again and again what we're about keeps that internal drive going and growing.

Missing a week or two from the band means you're missing a week or two of vision – and as the band grow and move forward, you're starting to get left behind. When vision doesn't remain fresh in you, the 'perishing' mentioned in Proverbs 29:18 starts, a withering away of your passion and motivation for what the team does, and is slowly replaced by a religious, duty-based, graceless, powerless drive, and after that a weariness and disillusionment. I've seen it happen in teams in the past, and I have no desire to see that happen in any of our teams.

Repeatedly hearing vision also helps to get that vision established in your own heart. When we hear something new, we go through various processes before it becomes part of us. First we question it, and then we weigh it against our previous knowledge, to decide if we'll pursue it further. The more we hear it, the more we start to understand it, and slowly it starts to become part of our thinking, and something we place value on. When we value vision, we begin to build our lives around it, our priorities change according to it. Then we start to impart that vision to those around us. It 'infects' everything we do, including and most particularly our leadership.

So coming to band night makes us better leaders.

Why do we have band nights?

PART 3

#rehearsal #practice

3. Rehearsal

This seems pretty obvious, but it's worth having a look at the purpose of rehearsal.

Rehearsal is not practice. Practice is something you do at home (or wherever) on your own to develop your skill and prepare yourself for when you're working with others. Practice will look different for everyone, but is something that should be part of our everyday life. We really do appreciate the hard work that everyone puts in with his or her personal practice – it does make a huge difference.

The dictionary defines rehearsal is the act of going through or recounting, in preparation for public performance. We are going over the songs we'll be using together, each bringing our own part, in readiness for Sunday morning. We know what we should be doing ourselves, now we just me to add it into the mix with everyone else, and make sure things slot together as they should. Where they don't it gives us the chance to creatively find new ways of making it work.

Rehearsal is our opportunity to keep what we play and sing submitted to the purpose and vision of the team and the worship leader. It's where we connect musically with each other, and with the songs themselves, making them come alive. Rehearsal reminds us that we are part of a greater whole, creating a synergy that is more powerful than if we'd tried to achieve the same individually. Rehearsal keeps us in communication with each other, makes us aware of each other's needs and strengths. It builds confidence in us individually and as a team, removes questions and concerns, and creates anticipation for the coming event.

Rehearsal enables us to prepare a platform from which we can lead on Sunday morning – a strong platform supported by trust, understanding, submission and excellence. It's like a clearing a roadway from rubble so that there are no obstacles or stumbling blocks for those travelling on the road:

Someone will say, 'Build a road! Build a road! Prepare the way! Make the way clear for my people'
Isaiah 57:14, NCV

nity

[I pray] . . . that they all may be one, as You, Father, are in me, and I in You; that they also may be one in Us, that the world may believe that You sent me.
John 17:21

The most effective a church, or a church team, can be is when they are in unity. There is the greatest power in witness and evangelism, and in any kind of ministry, when we are in unity. Jesus Himself knew that the most powerful way for the world to believe was by seeing the unity in His believers.

Unity is not something that comes naturally. It is a choice we all have to make, because it means laying aside personal opinions, preferences, even beliefs, for the sake of deciding to stand alongside each other. It's easy to stand alongside others we agree with, or like, or have similar ways of thinking. Not so much when there are disagreements, struggles, offences or personal agendas – that's when we need to make a choice to be above those things.

Our unity is built upon who Jesus is, not what we've done (well or badly), or what anyone else has done, or our preferences for church style or songs, or cultural or ethnic background. It's based on a simple decision to make Jesus the reason and the centre, even if it brings us into contact, and working with, people who we disagree with.

With that unity comes the promise of two things: 1) the world will know that Jesus is real and the gospel true; and 2) the glory of God will be so incredibly evident on us.

Unity is not a preference, feeling or 'spiritual leading' – it's a choice.

eflectors

#culture #beauty #commission

What a great word Pastor Andy brought at Vision Night this week[1].

Andy brought a fresh reminder that our role is to reflect God's glory, not take it. We are made to be beautiful, and to create beautiful things, but that beauty's purpose is to reflect God's beauty, not be glorified for itself. There is a culture within some of the Church, particularly in the West, to pursue worship ministry as our own ministry, a vehicle for our own purposes and ambitions. That culture creates a great-looking object that covers itself with the words and phrases of spiritual ministry, but at its heart is just a vehicle for personal ambition. The road to that culture starts when we get caught up in 'our gift', 'our calling', etc. God's calling always has been, and always will be, centred on the Church, His house, upon which has been placed His commission.

As Ephesians 1:23 says (in The Message), the world is peripheral to the church, not the other way round.

---

1 http://www.family-church.org.uk/creative/audio/visionnight_andyelmes.mp3; Vision Night was a night for all Family Church worship teams to meet together, three times a year. Pastor Andy Elmes is the senior pastor of Family Church.

In other words, it all starts with church – church is not something that is tagged onto us, particularly when it is convenient, or we have the blessing of the leadership. When we keep the God's house as the reason and centre for ministry, and remain submitted to God's purposes, we become reflectors in all we do. Though we look great ourselves, that beauty merely reflects God's incredible beauty, and all glory goes to Him.

Leadership

I believe everyone in the team is a leader. I've seen teams where people just show up and do a job; I've seen people try and hide on the stage while playing or singing; I've seen people put onto teams 'to encourage them' (ie. encourage them to keep coming to church!) or for inclusiveness; I've seen (too regularly) people finding the worship team as the outlet for their gift or talent.

I believe everyone on the worship team needs to understand that they are leaders, and that their behaviour and attitude on and off the platform has impact and influence. I believe that the more someone understands their role as a leader, the more their behaviour will change to match.

This belief affects everything we do on the platform. For instance, it's why we don't have music stands on stage – their size, and especially when there are many, creates walls that inhibits engagement with the congregation, allows people to hide or back off, and gives people an excuse for not preparing. Having reference tools like iPads and lyric screens is no problem, as they're discreet and unimposing. 'Hiding' is an easy thing to do on the stage, and it's the opposite of leadership.

A team of leaders in unity will not hide or back away. I believe a worship team should be bold, courageous and passionate in their leadership. That doesn't mean they are always loud or brash - it's about who they are not what they do. A worship team sets the atmosphere, and their example gives permission to the congregation to do as they do. Everything rises and falls on leadership, and becoming part of the worship team means accepting the responsibility of being a leader.

Let's choose to be leaders intentional about the way we lead, with selfless devotion to God's House and God's people, intentional about how we carry ourselves on and off the stage.

*T*he shout of redemption

#redemption #shout #praise #Balaam

Pastor Andy talked at our Vision Night[2] a lot about our sound – the sound of what God is doing in us. This sound isn't a particular style of music, or instrumental noise. It's something that sits deeper in the songs we use than the songs themselves. It's something that comes from our hearts, because it is a spiritual sound, not a soulish or physical sound.

In Numbers 23, Balaam has been asked by Balak, the king of Moab, to curse the army of Israel, as they were camped on Moab's doorstep and he saw no way to beat them. Whenever Balaam attempted to curse Israel he ended up blessing them, and in verse 20 and 21 he explains to Balak why:

> *I have received a command to bless; he has blessed, and I cannot change it. No misfortune is seen in Jacob, no misery observed in Israel. The Lord their God is with them; the shout of the King is among them.*
> **Number 23:20-21, NIV**

There was a shout in the heart of the nation, a

---

2 http://www.family-church.org.uk/creative/audio/visionnight_andyelmes.mp3

sound of praise that was beyond their songs but expressed their faith in God, their devotion and trust in Him that the fight they were about to enter into would result only in victory because God was with them. The sound that's in our house right now is the sound of redemption, a shout for the souls of the people in our families, workplaces, and communities. Our role as the worship team is to draw that shout out of our congregations, to not only influence the physical atmosphere through our music but to influence the spiritual atmosphere by our leading. That shout will be like a shield about us as we walk into our worlds with the story of redemption – like the Israelites, the enemy will not be able to stand against this weapon of unified praise.

Let the shout of redemption sound loud!

Redeeming worship

Here's another thought I want to pull out from Pastor Andy's message at Vision Night[3] last month: we as worship leaders are redeeming worship in the lives of our congregations.

The concept of worship in society, that we are all bombarded with, as that people are worthy of our praise because of what they can do, or what they look like. They are worthy to be upheld, respected, talked about, photographed and photoshopped, idolised and enshrined, all because of a talent, or lack of talent. It is a soulish-based expression of worship, motivated by emotion and insecurity; and we either slowly succumb to this shallow understanding of worship, or see the shallowness and harden our hearts against all forms of worship that have a hint of emotion in them. Our role as a worship team is to bring our congregation back from that shallow understanding to walking in a daily expression of intimate relationship through spiritual worship. We are commissioned in church to win back the hearts of God's people from

---

3   http://www.family-church.org.uk/creative/audio/visionnight_andyelmes.mp3

shallow, talent-inspired worship and draw them into a lifestyle of thankfulness, honour, devotion and sacrifice based on WHO GOD IS; worship that engages all that we are – spirit, soul and body.

We can't win people's hearts through being demanding or bossy, by firing out orders from the stage or by backing off and letting 'whatever goes' – that eventually leads to frustration and disheartenment. We first need to remember Who it is we are drawing them back to. It's not us, it is Almighty God, and all that He is. Yet, for others to see Him, they need to see Him through us. So our hearts must be devoted to Him, our service must come from a devoted and submitted heart to Him. All that we do must come from a heart of love, a desire to serve. That kind of lifestyle carries a fragrance that is not only pleasing to God, but also works on and pulls on the hearts of our congregations. It is the fragrance of God Himself on us that draws people, through us, to God.

We are redeemers in God's house, bringing His people back into a lifestyle and expression of worship that flows first from their spirit, out through their soul and their body.

*G*ive someone else the win

#surrender #Joab #David #leadership #humility

The heart of a worship leader is a heart of surrender. Similar to selflessness, but surrender is a decision we make when faced with the choice of our way or God's way. God's way can be presented either directly through Him speaking to us, but more often through what our leaders ask. The heart of surrender doesn't just wait until faced with that choice, it pursues the direction that will lead to our leader's request being the only way ahead.

Now Joab fought against Rabbah of the people of Ammon, and took the royal city. And Joab sent messengers to David, and said, "I have fought against Rabbah, and I have taken the city's water supply. Now therefore, gather the rest of the people together and encamp against the city and take it, lest I take the city and it be called after my name." So David gathered all the people together and went to Rabbah, fought against it, and took it. Then he took their king's crown from his head. Its weight was a talent of gold, with precious stones. And it was set on David's head. Also he brought out the spoil of the city in great abundance. And he brought out the people who were in it, and put them to work with saws and iron picks and iron axes, and made them cross over to

the brick works. So he did to all the cities of the people of
Ammon. Then David and all the people returned to Jerusalem.
2 Samuel 12:26-31

Joab was commander of David's army – he was trusted, had many people serving under him, was skilled and experienced, had a mind of his own and his own way of doing things. Here he had the opportunity to claim a win for himself, but it was more important to him that David be the one credited with that win. He understood that David was not just his 'boss', he represented Israel to the nations of the world; his reputation as king and leader affected how everyone viewed Israel.

It was more important to Joab that David looked strong and effective as king than he did as commander of the army. It was more important to him that David be seen being the one winning victories than himself. He realised that his authority as a leader came from David's kingship, not his own credibility or skill. He also carried no insecurity about his own position or how the men that served underneath him perceived him.

Pride would have said, "This win is mine, I did the work, I deserve to be acknowledged and praised for it." Instead, Joab pursued a course of action that put the win for him completely out of reach and entirely in David's hands.

Those who try to hold on to their lives will give up true life.
Those who give up their lives for me will hold on to true life.
Matthew 10:39 (NCV)

Whenever we try to hold onto a scrap of credit, we end up losing a piece of who we really are. To lose our life is not to lose our identity, as our identity is in Christ. We don't lose our personality or our skills or experience, but everything we are becomes grounded upon an unshakeable foundation of Christ being first in all things in our life.

Being surrendered does not make us weak or timid or quiet – Joab was bold and courageous to go up against a city and lead his army in it. We don't stop being who we are, but the source from which we draw our personality changes from being our own strength to God's strength. This stops insecurity, fear, doubt, jealousy – all things that will tarnish our leadership.

My own testimony

When I first started in worship teams, I was in a Baptist Church in Devon (I was about 18). We were preparing for a mid-week night of worship, and the worship leader had chosen songs, some of which were a bit old and done – that's what a lot of us thought, anyway – and so we complained about it, myself quite vigorously and spitefully.

The worship leader stayed calm and said that these were the songs he felt God saying to use. We broke off from rehearsal, and I wandered off, and got on my knees, and felt very clearly God say to me, "What do you think you're doing, how dare you? Who do you think you are?" I didn't 'hear' anything else but I knew that not only were the things I said hurtful and wrong, it was also not my place to have even questioned the song choice.

I could have pressed on with my own opinion, but I knew that wouldn't be right, and I just surrendered there and repented. Then I got up and apologised to the team leader, and said, "Whatever you want to do, I'm with you."

Something changed in me that night, and I still feel the effect of it now. I still have very strong opinions over song choice, etc., but I've learned firstly that there is an appropriate way to discuss these things with your leaders, but also that whatever is decided I will serve that choice and that leader wholeheartedly, and enable them to have the win.

Surrender is not the same as compromise. Compromise is something you do to keep a token of peace.

Surrender is your choice to give others the win.

Perishable things

For you know that it was not with perishable things such as silver or gold that you were redeemed from the empty way of life handed down to you from your ancestors, but with the precious blood of Christ, a lamb without blemish or defect.
1 Peter 1:18, NIV

It's easy in our 'style' of church to get caught up with how we do things so much that we tend to rely on that style too much. In truth, the lights, smoke, musicianship, staging, songs, etc. aren't going to save anyone. They are all 'things' that we use to create a pathway between the hearts of God's people to God's heart. Those things have a powerful effect on individuals and groups, so they can't be overlooked, ignored or belittled. But they are just things, and they will perish.

What matters most is what underlies the 'things' – that which comes from our hearts, that flows out of our spirit as we serve.

Wrong attitudes – selfish ambition, ego or pride, anger, bitterness, jealousy, negative talk – will infect and pollute what flows from the stage and weaken what we do together as a team. They leave us with only the 'things' we serve with to enable us to carry God's people and carry God's presence, and perishable things cannot carry or convey eternal truth and life. We all face situations where those kinds of attitudes can rise up within us – no one is immune from them. But we all have the ability to choose not to carry them in our daily life, and especially not to carry them into our teams and opportunities to serve others.

Great attitudes – faith, selflessness, joy, love, grace, encouragement, and anything that expresses God's life – are like platforms in our own life for God to speak and move in the lives of others. They carry life to others because they come from life – God's life. We lead strongly and effectively when the 'things' we use are empowered by life-giving attitudes. We know that salvation and redemption came to us when we had faith in Christ, and the sacrifice He made on the cross for us. For us to carry that redemption to others, our faith and reliance must continue to be in Christ alone, and not in the perishable 'things' we use.

*W*hich way is right?

#corporateworship #songs

The woman said to Him, "Sir, I perceive that You are a prophet. Our fathers worshiped on this mountain, and you Jews say that in Jerusalem is the place where one ought to worship." Jesus said to her, "Woman, believe Me, the hour is coming when you will neither on this mountain, nor in Jerusalem, worship the Father. You worship what you do not know; we know what we worship, for salvation is of the Jews. But the hour is coming, and now is, when the true worshipers will worship the Father in spirit and truth; for the Father is seeking such to worship Him. God is Spirit, and those who worship Him must worship in spirit and truth.
John 4:19-24

So let me be clear at the start of this series on Corporate Worship – I'm a worship leader and my heart is not for style, the latest songs, the coolest technology, or the current trends (or anti-trends) that regularly sweep the attention of the church this way and that. My heart is for people. In fact, I once saw a tweet that summed up my heart: "a worship leader is actually a people leader." I can't make you worship any more or less than you want to, but I can lead you by giving you a focus and direction, and creating an atmosphere where you can bring your worship as part of a congregation united in the same purpose.

The thing is, so much of how we 'do' worship in church these days is based around style or tradition; and each church will 'do' it differently, and each worship leader and pastor will secretly be thinking that they 'do' it better than most other churches around (yep, I can include myself in that!). I've been 'doing' this a while and I've come to the conclusion that God isn't really interested in what songs we use, or whether we have lights or not, or whether we have pews or cushioned seats. God is interested in people – that's what everything is all about, His love for people. So all these things (songs, technology, format, liturgy, etc.) that for each church help define who we are and how we operate, it's how we use them to serve people that matters to God, not that we have or don't have them.

Jesus's response to the Samaritan women makes it clear that God's heart is not for whether we do it this way or that, in this place or that, with lots of resources or none, but it is for authenticity and love in all that you do. Spirit and truth: an understanding that what we do is not just a physical thing but engages our lives with the presence of God and encompasses our whole being, starting from our inner person, our spirit, quickened and made alive by the life of Christ in us; and that before God all things are plain and open, nothing is covered, and anything that stands can only stand upon the foundation of His Word – everything else falls away and is exposed as empty before Him.

However we 'do' our corporate worship gatherings, they will only have value and spiritual integrity when we build them on the foundation of God's Word and a love for people.

*G*od is looking for you

#corporateworship #ready

But the hour is coming, and now is, when the true worshipers will worship the Father in spirit and truth; for the Father is seeking such to worship Him. God is Spirit, and those who worship Him must worship in spirit and truth.
John 4:23-24

There is so much packed into these few verses from John 4 about worship, but one more thing I want to draw out is this, from verses 23-24 – let's read them from The Message:

"It's who you are and the way you live that count before God. Your worship must engage your spirit in the pursuit of truth. That's the kind of people the Father is out looking for: those who are simply and honestly themselves before him in their worship. God is sheer being itself—Spirit. Those who worship him must do it out of their very being, their spirits, their true selves, in adoration."

Do you realise God is out looking for you, for us all? He's not passively sat by, waiting to see what happens in the hope that something might happen.

Imagine you've put on a big party – you're celebrating a significant birthday – and loads of people have come out to celebrate with you. The place is heaving with friends and family. The music kicks off and you want to dance (bear with me if you're not a dancer at parties, your imagination is key here!), so you head into the crowd to find some people who'll dance with you. But everyone you ask has some reason not to dance – they're not really into dancing, they don't like this song, they're talking to a long-lost friend. No one wants to dance with you (except for your slightly drunk Uncle who no one wants to dance with or be seen anywhere near to!) – how disappointed would you feel? But you keep looking around the room. Then you find someone, and then someone else, and so you start dancing, and maybe a few more come over and join you. But so many more are just milling around, maybe watching, maybe laughing at those dancing (especially the Uncle), maybe just not interested at all. It would seem strange to you that people who came out to celebrate with you aren't actually joining in with the celebration! Suddenly this party has become about what they want to do, and not about celebrating with you. Have you been to a party like that?

So maybe you're seeing where I'm going with this

already – that party sounds a little bit like church sometimes!

So let me say this again, straight from God's Word: He is looking for you! God is looking for people who will join with Him in His celebration. If you knew someone was looking for you, someone who you knew loved you and wanted to meet with you and enjoy your company, you'd do your best to get found by them. Let's not make excuses anymore for not joining in with God's celebration of His Son and our Saviour. Let's make it easy to be found by Him.

It all starts as a choice, the attitude we choose to come to church with, a decision that starts before we even get to church.

I was glad when they said to me, "Let us go to the house of the Lord".
Psalm 122:1

Come to church with a ready heart: ready to give, ready to serve, ready to join in. Prepare your heart before you leave your home.

*I*dentified as God's

#corporateworship #unity #identity

And it came to pass when the priests came out of the Most Holy Place (for all the priests who were present had sanctified themselves, without keeping to their divisions), and the Levites who were the singers, all those of Asaph and Heman and Jeduthun, with their sons and their brethren, stood at the east end of the altar, clothed in white linen, having cymbals, stringed instruments and harps, and with them one hundred and twenty priests sounding with trumpets — indeed it came to pass, when the trumpeters and singers were as one, to make one sound to be heard in praising and thanking the Lord, and when they lifted up their voice with the trumpets and cymbals and instruments of music, and praised the Lord, saying: "For He is good, For His mercy endures forever," that the house, the house of the Lord, was filled with a cloud, so that the priests could not continue ministering because of the cloud; for the glory of the Lord filled the house of God.
2 Chronicles 5:11-14

Here's the first of three important aspects of corporate worship that I hope will bring new life and understanding to your church worship.

Today's verses describe the dedication service of the brand new temple in Jerusalem, and is often quoted particularly during meetings focused specifically on seeking the outpouring of the Holy Spirit. The desire to have the same experience as the priests and ministers during this incredible moment of worship can be a strong focus and motivation for many of our meetings, but that's not the most significant part of this passage. In fact, I don't think it's the part we should be focusing on at all, especially for when we meet together.

The most significant part of this passage is what leads up to that overwhelming demonstration of God's glory, and that's what welcomed it into that service: unity in praise. Verse 13 says that 'it came to pass' that the 'musicians and singers were as one', to 'make one sound'. It didn't start off this way, but after a time there came a place of unity among everyone present; there was a oneness in them all. Now, I don't know about you, but I've noticed as a worship leader that oneness isn't something that happens naturally among humans! That requires a choice on the part of each of us – and that choice lays an incredible foundation for our corporate worship. Unity happens when we stop making church about our own individual purpose or desire, and instead make it about who we are corporately, together.

That's when God identifies us as His through the promise of His glory upon us:

Arise, shine; for your light has come! And the glory of the Lord is risen upon you. For behold, the darkness shall cover the earth, and deep darkness the people; but the Lord will arise over you, and His glory will be seen upon you. The Gentiles shall come to your light, and kings to the brightness of your rising.
Isaiah 60:1-3

What a great promise, when God's glory does come upon us. It isn't so that we can enjoy special moments in our meetings, but so that the whole world will recognise us as God's and will be drawn to us so they can meet with God. Even though people love darkness (and right now society is hurling itself headlong into greater darkness and separation from God), with God's glory risen upon us they will come looking for His light. That's not hopeful conjecture – that's God's promise.

But that comes when we make unity our focus and desire.

*A*n expression of love

#corporateworship #love #selfless

In the things I tell you now I don't praise you. Your meetings hurt you more than they help you. First, I hear that when you meet together as a church you are divided. And this is not hard to believe because of your idea that you must have separate groups to show who the real believers are! When you all come together, it is not really the Lord's Supper you are eating. I say this because when you eat, each one eats without waiting for the others. Some people don't get enough to eat or drink, while others have too much. You can eat and drink in your own homes. It seems that you think God's church is not important. You embarrass those who are poor. What can I say? Should I praise you? No, I cannot praise you for this. Before you eat the bread and drink the cup, you should examine your own attitude. So, my brothers and sisters, when you come together to eat, wait for each other. If some are too hungry to wait, they should eat at home. Do this so that your meeting together will not bring God's judgment on you.
1 Corinthians 11:17-22, 28, 33-34, ERV

To worship as a congregation – a group of people – requires us to be selfless, to consider others first. Sunday's meetings are not a social event, but a coming together of ONE body. They are not to 'top you up', but actually to empty you out! God cares about people, and it's not just the leadership's responsibility to care for people, it is everyone's.

Paul was not happy with the Corinthian church because they were treating the meetings very selfishly, serving their own needs and desires and ignoring others (particularly those who were in greater need). There was division because people cared more for their own opinion and self-importance. Some things never change!

Congregational worship is more than just a group of individuals individually worshipping. Church is not a place for you to express your own individual worship – it's not about you. Our attitude to church needs to be checked. Are we coming to 'get our own fill', 'to get our own experience of God'? Do we come in with self-importance, because of some revelation we think we have that makes us better? Do you think any of that impresses God?

Let's develop our personal, at-home worship life so that we don't come to church desperate to be filled or fixed. Let's avoid being self-indulgent, where our need to experience God at church crushes our desire to serve others. Church is about people, not you. Get your fix at home; don't depend on the church to give it to you. The heart behind Paul's chide was this: our attitude should be one of waiting on and serving each other. We belong to each other, so let's make church about other people, not ourselves. It's in the place of serving other's needs that we find our own needs met. It's in that place where we are helping others to engage with and experience the presence of God that we meet with God ourselves in a real, powerful and life-changing way.

And let us consider one another in order to stir up love and good works, not forsaking the assembling of ourselves together, as is the manner of some, but exhorting one another, and so much the more as you see the Day approaching.
Hebrews 10:24-25

Our corporate worship is for the sake of each other, not ourselves. Our hearts should be for each other: selfless, servant-hearted. Unity that comes from selflessness produces life.

May the God who gives endurance and encouragement give you the same attitude of mind toward each other that Christ Jesus had, so that with one mind and one voice you may glorify the God and Father of our Lord Jesus Christ.
Romans 15:5-6, NIV

A barrier and weapon against the enemy

#corporateworship #Balaam #shout #loudness

I have received a command to bless; he has blessed, and I cannot change it. No misfortune is seen in Jacob, no misery observed in Israel. The Lord their God is with them; the shout of the King is among them.
Numbers 23:20-21, NIV

Our corporate worship and praise is more than just a physical act of singing songs, or raising hands, or clapping or dancing. It is a spiritual thing, and works in ways we cannot see, but can sometimes feel. The spiritual darkness that has blinded the eyes of our communities continually resists the force of our worship because it understands and fears its strength and its source.

Today's verse comes from the story of Balaam, who had been commissioned by Balak, king of Moab, to curse Israel. Balak knew he needed a greater edge over Israel if he was to defeat them in battle, so he tried to use spiritual warfare. The problem was, every time Balaam tried to curse Israel it came out of his mouth as a blessing. He just could not curse Israel. The reason: 'the Lord their God is with them, the shout of the King is among them.'

There was something in Israel as a nation that resisted the spiritual curse. They weren't praying against Balaam; in fact, they had no idea any of this was going on at the time. They were just doing life, day to day, week to week, going to work, fixing the sink, teaching the kids, making bread, feeding the livestock. The outflow of their corporate praise, and their unity and sense of oneness and purpose as God's people brought a protection that they were completely unaware of. That's the power of corporate worship. Praise that started in the house of God destroyed the power of the curse, and that's still true today.

Loudness has been one of the most disputed issues in churches over the years, mainly because the spirit of religion that pervades much of how we worship together would seek to keep the people of God quiet as much as possible. There's nothing wrong with quietness – there are times when it is essential so we can hear God's voice and express depths of worship that are beyond words. But I'm not talking about individuals shouting, or wanting the freedom to be as noisy as they want (see *An expression of love*); I'm talking about a corporate loudness, a unified shout of praise. There is a shout waiting to be heard from us, that starts as a physical noise and becomes an incredible spiritual shout that causes strongholds to fall, prison walls to crumble, demons to flee, and God's glorious light to shine upon our communities.

Let's be bold with our praise when we come to meet together. Let's not allow self-consciousness, pride, or religious piety to rob us or our communities from the incredible, overwhelming, life-changing presence and glory of God that He desires to pour out over His people. Be selfless, look to serve and honour others, put aside personal preference in pursuit of a united expression of worship.

Let's let the shout be heard!

Team values: love

Let love be your highest goal!
1 Corinthians 14:1a, NLT

Love is our highest purpose

The worship team exists not to create music, but to serve people. The foundational value of our team is to love – as Paul says in 1 Corinthians 14:1, our highest aim, purpose and goal should be to love. That means first that we must make sure our highest goal is not:

- Artistry
- Musicianship
- Skill development
- Creating an atmosphere
- Sounding great
- Performance
- Using the latest songs
- Having a big team
- Having enough on the team
- Stage presence
- Using a broad selection of songs and hymns
- Not using music stands

All these things are important aspects of how our

team operates, and shouldn't be neglected BUT they are not as important as showing love to others. Love should be the motivating factor at work in everything we choose to do. For instance, love should be what determines:

How we treat our teams

Value them, value the time they give not just on Sundays but at rehearsals and in their own prep time. Value them by serving them and making sure they have all they need to serve the team and the church well. Love them by encouraging and drawing out the excellence that God has put in them rather than letting them drift into casualness. Honour them, and their families, with gratitude and care, knowing they are much more than just worship team members.

How we lead our congregation

Recognise that everyone is different, approaches worship differently, has come from different home experiences and different church experiences. Never lead or speak out of frustration, but always within your manner and speech keep a tone of love and care – that doesn't mean we back off or be patronising, or sappy, though! Looking and sounding good on stage is shallow and powerless if that is all you're aiming at

– it must be founded on the purpose of loving God's people and seeking to provide them with the strong, passionate, authentic leadership they need to step out of their own personal struggles and individual worship expression to come together as a united people, in agreement that Jesus Christ is Lord and He alone is worthy to be praised and worshipped, and that passionately and wholeheartedly. We are not apart from the congregation but a part of it, so we should never allow our performance of music to cause a separation – a congregation that thinks the worship team enjoys making and singing the music more than engaging with them will feel undervalued by the team, and disconnect and not be led. Similarly, a congregation that thinks the worship team doesn't really care about, or value, the music they play, or how they sing, or how they carry themselves on the platform of leadership they've been given, will feel that same sense of 'no value' toward themselves, and never feel encouraged to be led by the worship team.

It all hangs on love

Jesus said to him, "'You shall love the Lord your God with all your heart, with all your soul, and with all your mind.' This is the first and great commandment. And the second is like it: 'You shall love your neighbor as yourself.' On these

two commandments hang all the Law and the Prophets."
Matthew 22:37-40

Jesus told the Pharisees that everything that was important to them in their religious service and leadership – all the things that they valued as important in 'worshipping' God – were actually underpinned by two fundamental expressions of love that they had totally missed; love toward God and love toward others. Without love the things they valued and pursued wholeheartedly – even fanatically – were just shallow and meaningless, and meant nothing of significance to God.

It is so easy to value the creative aspect of our ministry – especially because we all love it so much anyway – that in our pursuit of it we end up devaluing or demoting the most important value we should hold as a team, to love others. The things we do, even the excellence and skill to which we do them, should be defined and formed by love, because without love they are empty, lifeless, showy, even self-indulgent. We should be excellent because we love those that will receive from our excellence. We should be exuberant and dynamic in our praise because we love God foremost, and we love those we lead so much that for them to see lackluster leadership would devalue worship for them. We should be diligent because we love the people on our teams and value their time and commitment. We should be selfless and defenceless in our own preferences and ideas because we love and value the inherent creativity in all our team members, and at the same time love our team members by giving them the strong, trustable leadership they need so that creativity has the security and safety, and direction, it needs to flourish.

Love changes everything

When we make love our highest pursuit and goal, it will change how we as leaders approach everything we do in and with our teams. It will affect how we choose to treat and lead our team members, and our congregation. It'll change our thinking about our stage presence and style of leadership. It'll shut down some avenues of creative expression, and open up whole new ones that require more effort but ultimately bear greater fruit in the life of our congregational worship. It'll be the deciding factor in decisions regarding style, song choice, people management, and commitment. It'll rattle the cage of lazy thinking, of religious thinking, and of super-spiritual thinking, exposing them for the selfishness that they really are.

Nothing we do as a worship team is more important than to love others. Without it we are, as it says in 1 Corinthians 13, just a bunch of noise. Even if the noise sounds tight and musically creative, it counts for nothing. The greatest way we can make sure that all that our team does is in strength and anointing is to make sure it is done with love. Love keeps all that we do as selfless and not showy; it keeps us from losing heart and focus, and empowers us through all circumstances, good and bad; it keeps our attitudes centred on Christ, it fuels our praise, and it never, never, ever gives up or fails. (1 Corinthians 13:4-7) Love is the strongest foundation we could ever build on.

Be intentional with love

Let's look for ways that we as leaders can be intentional in showing love to our team members and our congregation. Stop and pause over every idea and decision and consider what place love has in it. Give your team members the space and opportunity to find ways they can show love to others. Make the changes in your own leadership that you need to demonstrate to your team that you value them. Serve our congregations by being less caught up in the performance, and by removing the super-spirituality that tries to devalue the need for excellence.

Let's give the very best of ourselves to our team members and our congregation, purely out of love.

*H*unger for God in worship

What does hunger for God in worship look like? We could play a video from Bethel, with people passionately worshipping and crying out, and say 'That's hunger'; or we could play a video from a Pentecostal/Gospel church with people dancing in the aisles and say 'That's hunger'; or we could play a video from a prayer conference with people on the floor interceding passionately and say 'That's hunger'. All those things are outward expressions of hunger, but hunger itself is an inward motivation.

We could easily say hunger looks like this or that, or requires this or that expression or ritual, but those are all just 'things'.

In Matthew 22 the Pharisees tried to trick Jesus to find out what was the most important thing they did, and He said that none of things they did mattered when love was not present.

But when the Pharisees heard that He had silenced the Sadducees, they gathered together. Then one of them, a lawyer, asked Him a question, testing Him, and saying,

"Teacher, which is the great commandment in the law?"
Jesus said to him, "'You shall love the Lord your God with
all your heart, with all your soul, and with all your mind.'
This is the first and great commandment. And the second is
like it: 'You shall love your neighbor as yourself.' On these
two commandments hang all the Law and the Prophets."
Matthew 22:34-40

All the law hinged and rested on loving God with all your heart, soul and strength, and loving others. Nothing we 'do' – regardless of their biblical reference or denominational tradition – will cause us to be hungry for God, only what we choose inside. We can very easily find ourselves placing great value on the 'things' we do – and the heart of religion is to make that happen as much as possible – and forget or drift away from the underlying motivation that inspired that action in the first place.

Connected to eternity

He has made everything beautiful in its time. He also has
planted eternity in men's hearts and minds [a divinely
implanted sense of a purpose working through the ages
which nothing under the sun but God alone can satisfy],
yet so that men cannot find out what God has done from
the beginning to the end.
Ecclesiastes 3:11, AMP

We all have a yearning inside of us, because we are all made in God's image. Ecclesiastes 3:11 says that God has planted eternity in our hearts – we have a connection to something beyond this physical world that we see. CS Lewis, in his book *Mere Christianity*, explains it this way: if we find within ourselves a desire that no experience in this world could satisfy, then the most likely explanation is that we have been made for another world.

Start in the heart, consuming the whole

We are body, soul and spirit, as Paul writes in 1 Thessalonians 5:23:

> *Now may the God of peace Himself sanctify you completely; and may your whole spirit, soul, and body be preserved blameless at the coming of our Lord Jesus Christ.*

Psalm 42 – the writers (the sons of Korah) speak to all three parts of who we are throughout the Psalm. The physical afflictions being experienced – people ridiculing and condemning us; our soulish response to those experiences – we are cast down, distraught, reminiscent of times that we've walked away from; and our heart commands the direction we should take, that we should hope in God, declare praises to Him, not be dictated to by our soul.

As the hart pants and longs for the water brooks, so I pant and long for You, O God.

My inner self thirsts for God, for the living God. When shall I come and behold the face of God?

My tears have been my food day and night, while men say to me all day long, Where is your God?

These things I [earnestly] remember and pour myself out within me: how I went slowly before the throng and led them in procession to the house of God [like a bandmaster before his band, timing the steps to the sound of music and the chant of song], with the voice of shouting and praise, a throng keeping festival.

Why are you cast down, O my inner self? And why should you moan over me and be disquieted within me? Hope in God and wait expectantly for Him, for I shall yet praise Him, my Help and my God.

O my God, my life is cast down upon me [and I find the burden more than I can bear]; therefore will I [earnestly] remember You from the land of the Jordan [River] and the [summits of Mount] Hermon, from the little mountain Mizar.

[Roaring] deep calls to [roaring] deep at the thunder of Your waterspouts; all Your breakers and Your rolling waves have gone over me.

Yet the Lord will command His loving-kindness in the daytime, and in the night His song shall be with me, a prayer to the God of my life.

I will say to God my Rock, Why have You forgotten me? Why go I mourning because of the oppression of the enemy?

As with a sword [crushing] in my bones, my enemies
  taunt and reproach me, while they say continually to
  me, Where is your God?
Why are you cast down, O my inner self? And why should
  you moan over me and be disquieted within me? Hope in
  God and wait expectantly for Him, for I shall yet praise
  Him, Who is the help of my countenance, and my God.
Psalm 42, AMP

Horatio Spafford, whose daughters were lost to the sea in a shipping accident in the mid-Atlantic in the 1860s, made that the theme of his hymn *It is well with my soul* – in the midst of both peace and sorrow, blessing and hardship, my soul is well because it is led by my heart whose trust and hope is in God alone.

To be hungry for God in worship is to first allow our heart to be 'in command' – this is where our connection with eternity resides, this is where our desire and need for God begins. Our heart commands our soul, not the other way round (which is how it more often is because our soul is more dominant), our body outworks that expression through the physical acts described in the Bible: dancing, clapping, singing, shouting, raising hands, serving others. Too often we start by trying to command the acts first, by saying that it in doing so we are obeying God. But like He hated what the Pharisees stood for in their religious acts, God isn't touched by our acts alone, no matter how demonstrative or biblically-based they are.

Our worship starts in the heart and engages our whole being – Psalm 63:8 (AMP) says 'my whole being follows hard after You'.

Real unity in worship

But congregational worship is more than just our individual expression of worship, it is a unified declaration and enthroning of our God and King. When there is unity, there is blessing:

Behold, how good and how pleasant it is for brethren to dwell together in unity!
Psalm 133:1, NKJV

The American preacher AW Tozer describes unity in his book *The Pursuit of God* with the scene of one hundred grand pianos all together in a great hall – how do you get those pianos to all sound in tune? It's done by the piano tuner using the same tuning fork to tune each piano individually. The standard they are tuned to is the same for each piano – the single tuning fork. In the same way, unity amongst one hundred worshippers comes not when they agree with what each other believes or likes, but when each individual heart is tuned and turned toward Christ. They become closer to each other only when they become closer to God first, far closer than could ever be achieved if they were all to try to attain unity through their own efforts.

We can try to strive for unity but it'll never properly happen until it start when we set ourselves first to hunger after God and allow that hunger throughout our whole being. But when it does, the presence of God upon us as a people becomes tangible – 2 Chronicles 5:11-14 describes that unity that came about at the dedication of Solomon's Temple.

> *And it came to pass when the priests came out of the Most Holy Place (for all the priests who were present had sanctified themselves, without keeping to their divisions), and the Levites who were the singers, all those of Asaph and Heman and Jeduthun, with their sons and their brethren, stood at the east end of the altar, clothed in white linen, having cymbals, stringed instruments and harps, and with them one hundred and twenty priests sounding with trumpets—indeed it came to pass, when the trumpeters and singers were as one, to make one sound to be heard in praising and thanking the Lord, and when they lifted up their voice with the trumpets and cymbals and instruments of music, and praised the Lord, saying: "For He is good, for His mercy endures forever," that the house, the house of the Lord, was filled with a cloud, so that the priests could not continue ministering because of the cloud; for the glory of the Lord filled the house of God.*
> ***2 Chronicles 5:11-14***

And from that day the presence of God was a prominent and tangible aspect of the life of the temple, noticed by people all over the world so much that they would travel miles to experience it.

Don't wait to start at church

We can't make unity happen, it is a (super)natural result of when we each choose to allow our whole beings to be founded and directed by a hunger for God. When we worship it shouldn't be according to a tradition or style, or because that's what we're used to doing. Our worship shouldn't wait to start when the band kicks off the first song, it should be before we even leave for church – we should start releasing the desire and hunger in our inner self and allowing it to command our soul, in the midst of our circumstances, to hope in God, and our bodies to be ever praising Him.

$\mathcal{S}$tarted with a dream

#Joseph #dream #vision

Now Joseph had a dream, and he told it to his brothers;
and they hated him even more.
Genesis 37:5

Joseph has two dreams where he sees himself being bowed down to by his family. The road to leadership and walking in God's purpose for your life starts with a dream. God puts those dreams/thoughts/visions in our heart to start something off within us. It's a seed. Often we can think that the dream will come to pass exactly as we see it, and we don't understand or see the bigger picture, or what God is looking to achieve through us. It would be easy to make our lives all about fulfilling that dream.

Joseph's first dream is fulfilled in Genesis 42:6 but there's no way Joseph would have chosen the route he ended up taking to get there.

The vision/dream is a seed, showing God's purposes for you. But to walk in that vision requires God to do a work in you that means going through various experiences. Our attitude determines how quickly, deeply and strongly that work is done in us.

Joseph saw that God would bring him to a place of high rule over his family. It did not happen the way he thought it would – because he saw that vision within the confines of his own understanding and context. All he knew at that point was his family, so he saw the fulfillment of his dream just with his family.

When God gives us an understanding of our calling and purpose, we never see how it will actually be worked out; we couldn't. It is a trap to try and understand it within our current context and situation, as that will lead to frustration.

Ask God to make clear His purpose for you, but leave the fulfillment of it to Him.

*J*ealousy and Immaturity

#Joseph #jealousy #immaturity #dream

Now Joseph had a dream, and he told it to his brothers;
and they hated him even more.
Genesis 37:5

Often, when we see God's purposes for our lives, we get excited and want to tell others – it gives us a sense of placing and usefulness, and importance. Where there is insecurity in others, jealousy will often take hold. People around us won't necessarily understand our dream, because it portrays you as something bigger than what they know of you or think you could be.

We need to take care about who we share our dreams with. A vision is not a medal to be put on display, yet where there is immaturity it can often be used to establish significance over others. The vision is God's seed, so let that seed settle in your heart and take root, water it with prayer and feed it with God's word.

Joseph was young – about 17 – and already had a big head through the attention that he was given by his father. His immaturity caused him to misunderstand how to handle the dreams God had given. This fed the jealousy in his brothers' hearts. They sought to destroy him. There will always be people who seek to destroy your calling, who allow themselves to be used by the enemy to try and derail you from your purpose. But, what Joseph's brothers meant to bring death, God used to set Joseph off on his journey towards his real purpose.

We can't control the behaviour of others but we can exercise maturity: when we talk about our sense of godly purpose and when we respond to the behaviour of others. But also we must trust that God is working out His purpose in our lives, no matter what happens. Romans 8:28 says,

In all things God works for the good of those who love Him.

What the enemy used to destroy you, God will use to bring you further into His purpose.

$\mathcal{S}$old into slavery

#Joseph #vision #attitude

Now Joseph had been taken down to Egypt. And Potiphar,
an officer of Pharaoh, captain of the guard, an Egyptian,
bought him from the Ishmaelites who had taken him
down there.
Genesis 39:1

Joseph is sold to Potiphar, the captain of Pharaoh's guard. He demonstrates a good attitude and good ability, and finds himself promoted to household manager. Leaders are always looking for people who can do something well, and do it with a good attitude – no one wants a dead weight on their team! Joseph carried a sense of greatness and authority, but he was currently in a place where that greatness and authority was limited to someone else's vision.

There will be seasons where we find a degree of walking in our vision, where people see something on us and look to use what we can bring to enable their own vision. One of the best ways to see our own vision fulfilled is to serve and see someone else's vision fulfilled.

This is a season where we learn to develop our

giftings, where our character is developed, where we are faced with challenges and learn to overcome them. This is all part of the groundwork that God needs to do in us so that we can walk in a greater degree of calling.

But this season will always feel limited – because you're part of someone else's vision. It will always feel like not quite where you're supposed to be, even though you are experiencing blessing and growth. Just because we don't feel like it's quite the right place, we shouldn't rush to leave – it is all part of God's training for us. There are some valuable lessons for us to learn here, including not being led by our feelings and, more importantly, learning to submit to the leadership over us and staying within the boundaries set.

Joseph was given authority over everything in Potiphar's household except Potiphar's wife. When he was tempted to take more he refused. Understand that there will be boundaries to what you can do in this season. Though you may feel frustrated that you can't do more, don't let that frustration lead you to step outside or even leave.

In prison

#Joseph #limitations #calling #David

A t the end of Genesis 39 Joseph is unfairly thrown into prison. He could have taken that very badly, carried the injustice around with him, sought retribution. But he kept a good attitude – not a 'que sera, sera' attitude that just let's life steamroller over you, but a 'God is still in this, so I'll keep trusting Him' one. Joseph's attitude caused him to again rise to a place of authority, even in a prison.

Your calling is YOUR calling, and can't be taken away. You can try and run from it, like Jonah, but even then God will eventually catch up with you. No matter where you are, if you continue in faith and a good attitude, your calling will cause you to function in your gifting and anointing. There will be times when you feel even more restricted in what you can do, but often in those times you'll see new areas of your calling open up to you, a sense of greater power working through you.

Joseph knew he understood dreams because he'd seen what God was saying to him through his own dreams. He realised that the bales of hay in his first dream weren't actual bales of hay, but represented his brothers. Yet up until now we don't see any opportunity for that aspect of his gifting to be used. Now he's using that gift for other people, but not in a place that's very noticeable, not public.

When we walk with a sense of God's calling, our soul will attach a need for that calling to be noticed. We want to be used in that calling but we need people to know we have that calling so they can start using us in it. Again, that's a trap and will cause our calling to become established as a way of satisfying our own insecurity. God often puts us under great pressure in insignificant places to work in us a purity in our motives.

David's heart for worship began on a lonely hillside away from everyone else, forced to do things and be in places he didn't really want. Both David and Joseph could have reacted against their situations, got upset and angry – but nothing would have changed. Instead they found a growth in their heart for God and for His purpose in their lives.

It is often said that necessity is the mother of invention – really that means that when you are very limited in what you can do, you find new ways to find fulfillment. That wouldn't come without the pressure or limitation.

Positioned in God's timing

#Joseph #timing #dream

Finally, in Genesis 41, Joseph is not only released from prison, he is positioned in the authority and greatness that he sensed he was heading for all those years ago. Egypt at that time is the greatest nation on earth, and he is effectively put in charge of running it! He could not have got there without going through what must have looked at the time as going in completely the opposite direction or even it being called off well before it's time. And the various seasons he lived through worked in him a character and ability that prepared him to walk fully in his calling.

Then, in chapter 42, he sees one of his dreams come to pass – his brothers arrive to get food, and without knowing who he is, they bow before him. In chapter 46 his second dream is fulfilled when his father arrives in Egypt too.

Yet, having his family bow to him – which is what he saw in his dreams – was not what he was called to do. He was called to save Egypt, and his family, from a worldwide famine, and position the nation of Israel for its miraculous deliverance and identification as God's own people, paving the way for God's ultimate plan of redemption for all creation through His own Son, Jesus.

If Joseph had chased after just seeing his dream fulfilled as he saw it, he would have ended up trying to make his family bow to him through his own strength, and in his own timing (as soon as possible, probably!), which would have caused incredible resentment and hate, and would most likely have led to his brothers properly killing him.

When God puts a dream in our heart, it's not so we can see that exact thing get fulfilled. It's to cause us to start moving on a journey toward walking in His purposes for us. We cannot know what that journey involves – and if we did we'd probably walk away. What we end up walking in, when we allow God to lead us, is so much greater than what we first saw, and will have implications way beyond our own life.

What is your dream?
Take some time to pray and listen to God. What is it you see in your heart? Write it down. Just don't work out a five-step plan for how you're going to make it happen!

5 simple things you can do to grow as a worshipper in church

#church #worship #NewYear #heart #ready

The New Year is always a time to have a rethink, let go of some stuff and start something completely new. Your Facebook timeline is probably stuffed full of likes and shares of inspiring images and articles that give ideas for starting this New Year off proactively.

Since the bandwagon is already there to be climbed on, I thought I'd throw in a short article to help you make this year a year where you can experience a growing-up, so to speak, in your worship at church.

Worship itself is a lifestyle, a choice of how to live your life based on the values you hold in your heart – a heart that is redeemed and cleansed now by the great work of salvation that was won for us all by Jesus Christ at the cross. Those values are more than just preferences or likes, which reside in our soul – they are fundamental priorities, things of great importance, that define how we live, how we speak, how we behave and how we choose.

Proverbs 4:23 says:

Above all else, guard your heart, for everything you do flows from it.
Proverbs 4:23, NIV

So, with that in mind, here are five simple, starter ideas to help you grow in worship at church this year.

1. Start each Sunday, before you even leave for church, with a 'thank you'

Worship is directed always to God, and though our circumstances and feelings may changing radically (and often), He is unchanging – always good, always faithful, always reaching out to us, always waiting and ready when we turn back to Him, always true. Saying thanks helps us refocus ourselves back onto His unchanging nature. Saying thanks gets our faith going, that where all things around us seem to indicate otherwise, God has it in control, and it WILL end well. Saying thanks stops us from being self-focused, self-indulgent, self-anything, because it reminds us that it wasn't 'self' that saved us, but God alone.

Saying thanks before you leave for church gets your heart ready for what's ahead – ready to join with others in bringing praise to the name of Jesus, ready to make this coming morning about Jesus and His bride, the Church, and not about yourself.

2. Listen to some more worship albums

Singing is not in itself worship – it's just a way for it to be expressed. Yet it is an incredible way to express worship. There are studies after studies about music and singing, and their powerful effect on our whole being – body, soul and spirit. God designed music to be much more than just some notes creatively arranged in particular sequences. Musical worship is interwoven into the whole of creation – the Bible tells us even the rocks will cry out in praise, the trees and fields will shout and clap.

We're blessed these days to have access to a huge library of well-written songs from all over the world that is growing all the time. There's so much more available to listen to than what we use during the worship times at church. You can stir your heart to worship by listening to more worship music – and it's so easy to do nowadays thanks to the Internet (and I'm not talking about illegal downloading here!). There are many websites and services that stream music to your PC or smartphone/tablet – one of the most popular is Spotify. We have a Spotify playlist[4] for all the songs we use at Family Church, so you can listen to them again during the

---

4   https://open.spotify.com/user/fcworshipteam/playlist/5JTGyo6a1MaluzDCxSpSCx

week, as well as learn songs we're going to be teaching in the near future. You'll also find loads of albums and playlists, all free to listen to (if you can put up with the occasional advert, or fork up £10 a month for the premium version that cancels all adverts and gives you offline streaming too).

We are bombarded all the time with influences. Make a choice this New Year to shut down some of those influences and fill up instead with music written with the purpose of worshipping God.

3. Get to church early to say "Hi" to someone

Church is about people. Whether we know everyone at church or not, the reason why we have meetings is so that people can gather together. It's very easy, especially in larger churches, to just turn up, sing the songs, listen to the message, and go home – but that's missing the point of church completely. The word 'church' in Greek is *ekklesia*, which means "called-out ones". Not "called-out buildings", or "called-out organisations", but "ones": people. God is all for people, and His desire is for people to live together in relationships that demonstrate His love for all the world.

So, for this one, change your reason for coming to church and make it about connecting with people. Be intentional about it by coming a little earlier than the start of the meeting so you have a few minutes to say, "Hi" to someone. That makes your time at church purposeful rather than a duty or weekly habit.

It may be hard at first – some find it easier than others to even acknowledge the presence of someone you don't know! But saying, "Hi" is actually pretty easy – and that's all you have to do, to start with. Just say, "Hi". But do it intentionally, go early with the purpose of deliberately saying, "Hi".

4. Look for a way to bless or help out someone else at church each week

Following on from the last idea, make church about other people, not yourself. When we come to church with the desire to get what we want, we come with a selfish motivation. If the church meeting didn't please you or fulfill you in some way, was that because you came with only that intention?

It's actually an easy trap to fall into, to go to church each week looking to get blessed and inspired for yourself – and of course we do need to be being fed spiritually regularly. But coming to church with the intention of finding someone else to bless turns that motivation on its head and makes church a bless where people's needs are met because they've met someone else's needs.

That attitude of generosity has an effect on how we bring our own worship and how we worship together as a group. Proverbs 11:25 says that whoever gives generously will be refreshed. Yep, we all need refreshing at church, some weeks more than others. But God has designed church specifically so that what we need comes through someone else when we meet someone else's need.

5. Be standing up before the worship leader says "Hi!"

It's funny how doing one small thing has such a massive effect on what happens next. Yet, the simple, tiny choices we make in our heart before something that we know is going to happen, because it happens every time, happens can affect how we respond to that something.

The simple act of standing up before whoever is leading worship shouts out their introductory greeting demonstrates your choice to be ready. You're not waiting for someone else to get up before you do; you're not waiting until you're asked; you're not waiting until the conditions are conducive to your personal expression of worship, just the way you want it to be. Why wait? I mean, you know what coming already! Instead, choose to be ready to go. Choose because you're ready to worship. Choose because you want to worship. Choose because you know that God is more worthy than anything to be worshipped, and giving Him your thanks and praise is all you need to do right now.

That decision sets the path for the whole of the meeting for you. You're choosing to worship, not just following along. You're choosing to praise, not just sing along with the songs. So many of the verses in the Psalms – a book packed full of expressions of praise and worship – start with the words "I will...". That indicates a choice, an intention, a decision. Your choice to worship isn't (or, at least, shouldn't be) based on what songs the worship team are using each morning, but on who God is – His nature, His promises, His love.

Starts in the heart

All of these ideas are heart-based actions. They aren't based on how you feel, or what you're currently going through. Worship, though something that engages our whole being, starts in our hearts.

These are just five simple ideas to get you going. There are plenty of other things you can do to take your engagement in worship at church to a new level. Maybe you can think of some yourself?

New Year thoughts

#NewYear #growth #vision #harvest

At the end of last year I shared a message to our whole worship team for the coming New Year. Although it was written for our team, and particularly for where our church is going in this New Year, I'm sure there will be something there that will encourage and inspire you too – at least, that's my hope in sharing it with you!

Have a great New Year and, letting go of the things of last year, hold fast to the prize of the upward call of God, which is Jesus Christ Himself (Philippians 3:13-14).

Thanks

First off we want to say a massive thank you to all of you for your heart, passion and tireless service over this year. It is a great pleasure to be serving alongside you all because you are such an exciting, creative and inspiring bunch of people!

We have so much to be thankful for as a team. This last year has seen real growth, not just with seeing a new congregation launched, but each congregational team becoming stronger in leadership. There are always challenges, there always will be, but it is in facing those challenges head-on and seeing God make the way for us, bringing the provision and breakthrough we need, that the real growth takes place. One of the key 'doorways' into worship is giving thanks, and for us to lead others in giving thanks we need to maintain an attitude of thanksgiving ourselves. Breakthroughs and provisions come when we start by giving thanks. Let's go into this New Year with thanks in our hearts and on our lips what God has done already and what He is about to do.

> *Giving thanks always for all things to God the Father in the name of our Lord Jesus Christ.*
> **Ephesians 5:20**

Spiritual Growth

Worship is a spiritual thing; more than an 'act', it's the flowing out of God's life within us into and through every area of our lives, redefining our values and priorities around God. Leading worship is more than us just singing and playing carefully chosen songs with enthusiasm and passion. We are leading a spiritual flow of life from our congregations, out of our own spiritual flow of life.

"He who believes in Me, as the Scripture has said, out of his heart will flow rivers of living water." But this He spoke concerning the Spirit, whom those believing in Him would receive; for the Holy Spirit was not yet given, because Jesus was not yet glorified.
John 7:38-39

I'll bring You more than a song

Let's make this year a year where we prioritise and pursue a deeper spiritual foundation for our ministry. It's one thing to make a song sound good through dedicated musicianship and vocals, but those things are the natural aspects of what we do, and we can't lead something spiritual with something that is natural. We don't ignore good musicianship – a deeper spiritual pursuit will inspire us to make sure our natural abilities can carry and enable our spiritual vision. But a song played well won't be enough to lead people to worship from their spirit.

More of His Word

In this New Year, let's give more time to our relationship with God, to reading His Word. Let's give time on our own and during our team nights to pray and intercede for our congregations, praying the Word of God over them, and speaking the Word over them as we lead them.

*And take the helmet of salvation, and the sword of the
Spirit, which is the word of God.*
Ephesians 6:17

The Word of God is our spiritual sword, that makes
the difference between soulish and spiritual; it is where
our strength comes from, where our wisdom as leaders
flows from, where our refreshment from tiredness
and dryness pours from.

*For the word of God is living and powerful, and sharper
than any two-edged sword, piercing even to the division
of soul and spirit, and of joints and marrow, and is a
discerner of the thoughts and intents of the heart.*
Hebrews 4:12

We grow stronger in spiritual leadership by knowing
God's Word; and, we avoid our leadership becoming
soulish by knowing God's Word.

Rooted in spiritual strength
Our vision is to carry God's presence to His people,
and to carry His people into His presence, through
character and creativity. We do that through all three
aspects of human experience – body, soul and spirit
– because worship engages all three areas. But it starts
in the spirit. That's what God is looking for.

"But the hour is coming, and now is, when the true worshipers will worship the Father in spirit and truth; for the Father is seeking such to worship Him. God is Spirit, and those who worship Him must worship in spirit and truth."
John 4:23-24

Our leadership is rooted in our spiritual strength, not our natural ability.

Reaping a spiritual harvest

This New Year is a year for greater spirituality – not weird, or flaky, or hokey, but rooted in God's Word. Our congregations need us to lead with greater spirituality. Our communities need to see a church that is spiritual and not weird or shallow. Greater spirituality in our lives and leadership will bring a desire for deeper worship in our congregations as we lead them. The harvest of that will be a church that lives out a worship life beyond the Sunday morning meetings that we hold, a worship life that carries God's presence into our communities and sees His kingdom established there.

"And I [Jesus], if I am lifted up from the earth, will draw all peoples to Myself."
John 12:32

Let's take up that responsibility this year. It's in our hands as leaders. God has equipped us and anointed us with His Spirit, His power, His promises. What an exciting time to be leading worship!

The platform we build

A platform is the opportunity to influence another life.

We must be careful not to build a platform on talent. We may impress people with our talent, but it doesn't change anything in their life, and their connection with us is shallow, and will change the moment we play a wrong note, or have an off day.

Our platform is one of selflessness – we influence others through serving them. Selflessness comes from our hearts and connects us with our congregation at a heart level.

Every Sunday we are given a platform. It is not ours, we don't own it, but we use it submitted to those that gave it to us. It was not given to us to serve our purposes but for us to serve others. How well we use it depends on the mindset we each bring to it. The right mindset enables us to reach out and touch people's lives; a wrong mindset will try and pull everything that happens into our own agenda and preference.

For Solomon had made a bronze platform five cubits long, five cubits wide, and three cubits high, and had set it in

*the midst of the court; and he stood on it, knelt down on
his knees before all the assembly of Israel, and spread out
his hands toward heaven.*
2 Chronicles 6:13

Solomon dedicates the new temple and builds a
platform in the midst of the people, where he humbles
himself and surrenders to heaven, and prays a prayer
of dedication that leads to an incredible outpouring
of God's presence in the worship that follows.

*So Ezra the scribe stood on a platform of wood, which they
had made for the purpose; and beside him, at his right hand,
stood Mattithiah, Shema, Anaiah, Urijah, Hilkiah, and
Maaseiah; and at his left hand Pedaiah, Mishael, Malchijah,
Hashum, Hashbadana, Zechariah, and Meshullam. And
Ezra opened the book in the sight of all the people, for he
was standing above all the people; and when he opened
it, all the people stood up.*
Nehemiah 8:4-5

Nehemiah builds a platform for the purpose of
reading God's Word to the nation. He is surrounded
by his fellow priests. The whole nation understands
the importance of what he does, as they stand to their
feet the moment he opens the book, in readiness to
hear and respond.

Platforms bring a focus to leadership, but they are

built for a purpose beyond that of the one who stands on it. Let's have Solomon's attitude of surrender, and Nehemiah's attitude that what we're here for is more important than our own purpose.

Living out of our new nature

Andy's great message from Sunday – "Live out of your new nature" – makes what we do as a team pretty simple, really. Because, when it comes down to it, skill level or experience or knowledge or talent will never trump or be a more powerful force in our ministry and leading than the nature of God at work in and through us.

So this might sound really obvious and simple, but this is how we as a team will move forward in leading the church in worship – by living out of our new Christ-like nature, and not our old soulish, insecure, "I need my opinion to be heard", do-it-my-own-way nature. If we as a team can grow in our understanding of who we are in Christ, and serve out of that – and not out of our skill, knowledge or experience – then our church will feel that coming through in the worship we lead, and will want their own worship to move up to that level.

Andy's messages about our new nature are ones we need, as a team, to grab hold of and allow the Holy

Spirit to imprint His word on our hearts through them. Christ is the centre of all we do, and it has to be His nature that flows out through what we do, and not anything else.

Blowing your own trumpet

Most men will proclaim each his own goodness, but who can find a faithful man?
Proverbs 20:6

This verse came up in the Faith Works Bible School notes tonight, and it made me think how easily we can blow our own trumpet when we want people to know about what we can do or have done, but that actually what God always looks for is the one who can just get on and serve, and do it regularly and consistently, without the need for applause or reward.

Being faithful means being selfless. There's no glory or praise or thanks in being faithful, generally speaking. You're faithful because that's who you are.

Faithfulness is a characteristic of God, so when we choose to be faithful, we find we walk in God's character and strength, not our own. We enable the character of God to be seen through us, and His power to work through us.

Anyone can talk about what they can do or have done, but God is looking for gifting or achievement to serve Him and build His kingdom – He's looking for faithfulness. Always being there, always preparing, always serving, always submitted to vision, always speaking positively and walking consistently and with integrity.

Your walk should be doing the talking!

Getting the WHY and the WHAT the right way round

#motivation #calling

I've often heard people say, "God has called me to lead worship". I've often heard it spoken by people who have designs on being the next Matt Redman or Darlene Zschech. I've also known many people who have served on worship teams who've never expressed a sense of calling to that specific ministry. I didn't have any sense of calling to leading worship until a few years into being involved in a worship team. What I've realised over the years, though, is that actually our calling is far broader than any specific ministry.

2 Corinthians 5:18 says that God reconciled us to Himself, and has now given us the calling or ministry of reconciling others to Him – because God's greatest desire is that ALL should be saved. Jesus did all that was necessary – His blood poured out as a complete and whole atonement for our sin. Now our calling is to see that worked out in our world.

It's not about what specific ministry you feel called to: it's about WHY. Why do you want to serve, why do you want to lead, why do you want to play? Once we understand what God has done for us, the motive for all we do becomes one of self-sacrifice for the sake of seeing others reconciled to God.

When we make it about any specific ministry that we want to do, we've lost sight of the real WHY. Sure, we're given certain gifts, talents, skills, and 'fields of specialised ability' – but we shouldn't define our service by them, they should empower our service to reconcile more people.

I once heard an interview with Billy Graham where he said that he has never once felt any sense of calling to be an evangelist, he just had this overwhelming urge that people needed to hear the Gospel because he knew it could change their lives, and he responded by doing what he knew – to tell as many people. He realised along the way that he was actually quite good at being able to communicate truth simply and effectively!

The WHAT tends to get itself sorted once you have the WHY right.

No turning back

Last week I wrote about our calling – that although we may think we have quite specific callings, we're ALL called to the simple purpose of reconciling people to God, through the redemptive and final work of the cross.

> *And they shall rebuild the old ruins, they shall raise up the former desolations, And they shall repair the ruined cities, the desolations of many generations.*
> **Isaiah 61:4**

This verse follows straight on from the verses, quoted by Jesus, that speak of God's Spirit being upon us to heal, restore, release and bind up. The very heart of God's kingdom is what He can do through us to help others. Our lives, being not our own anymore, are being moulded by God to be not just a workmanship of His grace, but also an outworking of His grace to the world.

God loves restoring things that the world says are unrestorable, derelict and without hope. We have a part to play in that restoration when we lead corporate worship. On one level, the words that we sing tech people truth about Jesus, the cross, God's love, grace and power. But on a deeper level, our own surrender to God's redemptive power and our pursuit of a life lived to serve God's kingdom purposes – deciding to follow Jesus, no turning back – brings an anointing on our songs, the Holy Spirit's healing, restoring, releasing noticing that works in people's lives regardless of the words we're singing.

A musically and technically good team can do well, but a team made up of people who are fully sold out to the call of 'No turning back' is unstoppable.

Guess what kind of team we're building here?

New every day

Great is his faithfulness; his mercies begin afresh each morning.
Lamentations 3:23, NLT

Every day is a new day in God. There is something new that God has for you every day. Every day is different because every day there's something new. What was new yesterday is no longer new, and God has something that is new for you today.

Maybe you didn't quite pick up on it, but the point I wanted to make was this: Every day is a NEW day with God. New. Not rehashed from yesterday; not revived from the 80's; not revamped from yesteryear; not restored from history. New. Never been before. Not seen previously. New.

Okay, I've made my point. The thing I want to focus on here – and there's so much I could focus on with that truth – is that when we come to leading our church on a Sunday morning, we need to remind ourselves that this gathering, this congregation, has all the potential and possibility of being something completely new, different to last week, or last month, even if the songs were all the same and the message was the same. It'll be new because on that day God has new things that He didn't have waiting for us the week before.

It's easy to come along to church with a "Here we go again" mindset, where we know the form, the run list, the timings, the transitions and turnarounds. Probably a lot of our church congregation comes with that mindset; probably even most churches across the country do. Why? Because we so easily settle into routine and structure. Routine and structure are good, but not when they become the 'road' we travel and the 'engine' that drives us down it.

Let's keep reminding ourselves that, "Hey, today is completely new, it hasn't been seen before."

What new things does God have for His church today?

Repetition

#practice #meditate #strength

Repetition is one of the surest and strongest ways to grow, in anything – as long as that repetition has purpose, and is not treated as just 'ticking a box'

Spiritually

First of all, for our spiritual growth, the Bible talks often about meditating on God's word or law – that literally means to chew over and over, to read and re-read and re-read again. We read a passage, and we understand the words that have been used, or at least most of them. After another read we get a better understanding of the context. Then we start to understand more of a practical application for our lives. Then God hits us with a revelation that opens our eyes to more of who He is.

Naturally

Our musicianship (and I include singing in that) develops through repetition. We don't just learn a phrase or chord run, and we're done with it – repetition allows us to first become grounded in the basic of the music, then make sure we get the timing right, then understand how we could give better tone to the notes, then maybe explore other ways of doing the same thing. We're not just learning a piece of music, we're making that music take shape and have life.

Repetition sounds pretty boring or mundane, no glory or excitement. Actually, it's in repetition that we become stronger. When a muscle is developed through exercise, it's the repetition of the same exercise that first loosens the muscle, clears out the kinks, and then builds strength. It's easy to ignore the mundane because our souls desire excitement and glory. But it's in the mundane that our character is formed.

Let's make sure our repetition, natural and spiritual, has a purpose and a goal.

*W*hen you're not feeling it

What do you do when you feel like you have nothing – nothing inside you, no urge, no motivation, no desire?

Everyone goes through times – for various reasons – where we just aren't feeling it; we'd rather just sit on the sides and watch. It isn't wrong to feel like that, but it is wrong to let those feelings stick around and become the norm. It's how we deal with it, how we choose to respond, that makes the difference. And we as leaders have to learn the right response and keep choosing it, so that we can lead others who are in a similar place. When we learn to get the victory in these times it adds something to us on the inside, and that something comes out when we lead worship.

First we need to get our perspective right, on whatever the situation is, and that means putting God first in it and seeing, regardless of the perceived hopelessness of it, that God is with us and will honour His promise to bring His purpose out of it. God is at the centre of it all, and is the head of it all. That's where we start.

Then we need to start giving thanks.
1 Thessalonians 5:18 (NIV) says:

[Give] thanks in everything, for this is God's will for you in Christ Jesus.

God wants us to give thanks, no matter where we are. Giving thanks continues to change our perspective – it helps to not only focus our sight on God, but also to increase our sight, so we see beyond where we are now and how we feel now. Psalm 103:2 (and the following verses) give us the starting point, reminding us of all that God has already done for us. This stuff is done, it's fixed, unalterable, and now it's about to be outworked in your life. Reminding ourselves of these things helps us to remind our congregation when they need reminding – we encourage them with the truth we know rather than just saying words that are empty.

Then we need to keep encouraging ourselves to continue. The 'praise the Lord, O my soul' in verse 2 of Psalm 103 is not just a suggestion – it's a personal command, a push to keep on going. If we are to be able to give our congregations that extra push they need to continue to praise God boldly, it has to come from us having already pushed through.

What things do you do to help you push through?

Pruning

Sometimes it can feel like everything you've come to rely on is being taken away from you; everything that you thought made what you do strong is suddenly no longer there. It would be easy in those times to panic, fret, and make knee-jerk decisions. It would be even easier to just quit and walk away.

These times are actually very significant times, because God, the gardener, is pruning you. In John 15:2, Jesus says that the Father prunes and cuts back any branch that is bearing fruit. That's a good thing, because in pruning the branch, it can bear even more fruit.

We've been doing well with what we have, but now God wants to do even more through us. Our trust stops settling on the resources we've had available to us and is restored back to being in Him alone. Where we once bore good fruit, we now start to bear great fruit, and more of it.

Growth means submitting ourselves to the process of pruning. It can be painful and worrying to go through, and can often look to outsiders that we've lost it completely, but it just a short season, and then comes the growth that God saw right from the start.

If/when you're being pruned, that's the time to be thankful that God is working on your behalf right now, and very soon you'll see the blossom that is the promise and hope of brand new fruit in your life.

Coming to church to get, or to give?

#giving #selfless #church

In 1 Corinthians 11:17-33, Paul disciplines the Corinthians about their attitude towards worship and sharing communion together. He describes a picture of self-indulgence cloaked in religious fervour. It's a sad state for a church to be in, but I wonder if we see the same attitudes in churches now in regard to worship.

We may not see fights breaking out over the trays of bread as they get passed around the church, but maybe that self-indulgence has got into our thinking about how and why we come to church in the first place. Are people coming for what they can get out of church, and placing a demand on church for a greater spiritual experience – an experience that actually we should be finding in our own daily walk with God, not at a Sunday morning meeting? Maybe!

In Paul's correction to the Corinthians, he tells them to 'wait for each other' – in other words, when we come to worship together, it shouldn't be about getting our spiritual fix and feeling like we've got what we wanted out of church, but we should selflessly serve and honour each other and make sure that everyone else is able to engage with what the whole church is doing.

When we come together as a congregation, something takes place that goes way higher than what we could experience individually. In worshipping together, we worship as the body of Christ, bought by His blood. We are one body, and the oneness should be expressed in all aspects of our church life. Communion, as described by Paul in 1 Corinthians 11, is a picture of that.

This thought is a kick-starter – it's unfinished because there's so much more to say, and it can't be said in just one small email message. But the start of it is this thought/challenge: are we coming to church to get, or to give?

To lead someone in you have to lead them out

Getting the nation of Israel into the Promised Land was a massive job for Moses, but it started with the massive job of getting them out! Before they could cross the Jordan, destroy Jericho, and start growing their own food and building their own houses on their own land, they had to leave Egypt. That involved a series of miraculous plagues, a chase across the desert and deliverance in the Red Sea. To get the Israelites into Israel, Moses had to get them out of Egypt.

Our vision as a team is to lead God's people into His presence. But to do that we need to lead them out – out from under the weight of their circumstances, out from the anxieties and hassles that are dogging their thoughts, out from the sense of failure of not having lived right during the last week – there is so much that people carry with them, and we are a part of leading them out of that captivity into the freedom of God's presence.

Praise is such a powerful key to bringing people out of captivity:

- Praise caused the walls of Paul and Silas' prison to crumble (Acts 16:16-40).
- Praise caused the walls of Jericho to fall (Joshua 6).
- Praise caused the enemy to flee and destroy itself (2 Chronicles 20).
- Praise lifts off heaviness (Isaiah 61:3).

Praise is a liberator, and strong praise is how we lead people out ready to lead them in. The devil hates strong praise, because he knows its power; but there is nothing he can do to stop the flood of God's presence when the banner of praise is lifted up with boldness.

And that's what we need to do – lead out the praise with boldness. And I don't just mean the first praise song of a Sunday morning, although that is very important. Whenever we lead people in worship, wherever it is, we must bring praise, be bold with it, and draw bold praise from the people we lead. People need to praise – and we need to be bold in leading it.

Worship is led

The best worship leader in the world is you. You know you; you know whether you're engaging or just being tokenistic; you know if you're giving your all or just following a set, learnt pattern.

You are the best worship leader you could ever have. Chris Tomlin or Joel Houston could do a pretty good job for you; Jesus Culture would do well; but not as well as you could yourself.

Take a look at a pretty dark time in David's life:

> *Now David was greatly distressed, for the people spoke of stoning him, because the soul of all the people was grieved, every man for his sons and his daughters. But David strengthened himself in the Lord his God.*
> **1 Samuel 30:6**

David's position was desperate – he'd lost his home and his family, and his friends and colleagues were about to turn on him. Out of all the possible options available to him, he chose to lead himself in worship. He didn't turn to the priest, or one of his trusted advisers or most skilful musicians – he did it himself.

Are you able to lead yourself in worship, or do you rely on having others do it for you? We can't lead others where we haven't been ourselves. David learnt to lead himself in the private place, out in the fields tending and protecting his family's sheep. He learnt where no one was looking, and not because it would help him in later life but because he wanted to know God more, and his desire was for God above all else.

Take the lead and lead yourself – what's holding you back?

Where does our confidence come from?

#confidence #character #authority

I used to be very nervous standing in front of a crowd of people who were looking at me (I'm not totally comfortable with it even now!), and when I started playing in a worship team 20-something years ago I would keep very much in the background, with my head down, not paying anyone any attention!

As I started leading worship, and studying and seeking God to grow as a leader, I began to learn more about where my confidence should come from, and why, and this has changed completely the way I am when I lead people in worship, regardless of the size of the crowd or who's in it.

It's easy to feel uncertain or nervous when we place ourselves in front of people and endeavour to sing or play and lead them in worship. Will I be accepted? Will they like what I do? Will they think me arrogant or full of myself? Will they laugh at me? All those thoughts and more go through our minds, undermining our confidence.

But what makes the difference is when we understand

where our confidence really comes from, and that we are there with authority – God-given authority. We have been given God's authority to lead His people – it's not our own, it's ours because we submit ourselves to His authority, and to our leaders. We can be confident because it is God at work in and through us, not our own ability, which is causing the hearts of the church to respond with worship.

Authority is carried by character, not talent/skill. God's authority sits on the shoulders of our character like the mantel that Elijah passed to Elisha. Elijah was God's prophet – His voice and authority – to the nation of Israel, and when he was taken up to heaven, Elisha took the Prophet's mantel on himself and began to walk in the same authority that Elijah walked in – in fact, he took it further and believed God for a double portion of Elijah's authority (2 Kings 2:9-14). The mantel (or cloak), to Elisha, was a symbol of God's authority on him and he confidently served the nation of Israel through it.

God's authority is a gift, so it's on us to develop our character to be able to carry it. What are you doing in your daily worship life to keep developing your character?

Face the fear

When I was in New York City a while ago I visited the Empire State Building and took the ride up to the outdoor viewing gallery – eighty-six floors up! For those that know me, this was not an easy thing for me to do. I've not done well with heights AT ALL since as long as I can remember – even looking down from a couple of floors up can make me feel weird. But I was determined to go all the way up and take in the legendary view of Manhattan. I took my time, didn't move too quickly, breathed deeply, and chose to enjoy it all. A week later we were a few floors up in a not un-often-visited furniture store, and I looked down out of the window and felt no weird height sensation at all. Not even looking down over the balconies, or up from the bottom floor. It's like my brain decided that actually, if I can handle the top of the Empire State Building, then a few floors up is really no problem at all. Facing my fear of heights brought me to a place of new strength.

It's natural for us to keep away or run from uncomfortable, difficult and even painful situations.

No one desires or wishes those situations on themselves or anyone else, but they come – and it is our attitude toward them that affects how we change, or don't change, after they pass.

The writer of Romans says that, rather than shying away from difficulty, or tribulations, "we . . . glory in [them], knowing that tribulation produces perseverance; and perseverance, character; and character, hope" (Romans 5:3, 4). The prize for facing and persevering through difficult situations is greater character and renewed hope.

That character is what enables us to walk in the greater levels of influence and opportunity that God has prepared for us. Talent won't do that, reputation or previous experience won't do that. It's what is in your heart that has formed your attitudes and values, and that keeps you in God's ways when you walk in uncharted territory.

Whatever we are facing, God's promise is that He is always with us.

Honour

#honour #values

Honour is an outward expression of the worship life that we live. It is an outworking of character. Honour says more about who you are than it does the person or people you are honouring.

Romans 12:10 says "Honour one another above yourselves." This instruction comes in the middle of a whole conversation regarding the way we should live our lives, that starts with the call to lay our whole lives upon the altar of worship, which is our 'reasonable act of worship'. To honour others above ourselves is a choice, and comes at a price – laying ourselves down and seeking God's purpose in our everyday lives.

It's easy to honour people who, to our perspective, have worth because of what they have done or the position they hold. It's not so easy to honour those that we find it hard to get along with. But how we life out a worship life is not based on how other people act or behave, but on our own revelation of God in our life. We honour others because we are honourable people, not because others live in a manner worthy of honour. We honour others because we honour God, and God's values are higher and of greater purpose than our own opinions or values, or what we deem 'right'. If our lives are missing that element of honour then our worship is shallow, and based only on what we like or enjoy.

Generational

Pastor Andy shared on our twelfth church value last Sunday: Generational. Not only does what we bring to the team affect what's happening in our church now, it has an impact on where our church is going in the years ahead, as the next generation watch us, mimic us, learn from us and then take over from us. The purposes we serve in God's kingdom now will continue long after we've finished our race, but when we do pass on the baton we must ensure we pass it on to a generation who are stronger, wiser and more passionate than we were when we took the baton ourselves.

David, in 1 Chronicles 22, knew that he couldn't build the temple himself, yet he carried the vision for the temple in his heart. He knew what the cost would be, he knew what was needed, he knew what it should look like, and he knew what effect it should have on the world:

> *We should build a great temple for the Lord, which will be famous everywhere.*
> **1 Chronicles 22:5, NCV**

So not only did David gather all the resources ready to build the temple, he imparted the vision for the temple into the heart of his son Solomon. When Solomon built the temple, he wasn't just building David's idea of the temple; it had become his idea, his vision.

That's how being generational works. What is passed on is not just 'a tradition to be maintained', or a set of rules that must continually be adhered to – but a heartbeat, a passion, that is owned by each generation; that inspires and motivates each generation even though the circumstances change, or the resources change, or the styles change.

Let's never forget that we are being watched, that there are young people starting to question and learn and form their understanding by watching us, and learning from us. We want to see that generation go further than we ever could. This world needs a generation that is not insecure, or ego-driven, or passionless – it needs a generation that has society-impacting integrity and passion, that has a strong sense of identity and purpose. They'll learn that from us, and they'll take it further.

I'm coming out!

What a fantastic weekend we've just had! A massive thanks to everyone involved in leading worship over the weekend, whether at the Kings Theatre or at our congregations on Sunday.

This weekend has been all about coming out of our box, breaking through the limitations that we've held over ourselves either through fear or things others say, or perceived lack of resources. This has to be something we as worship leaders are seeking to do, because any limitations we put on ourselves we will also put on our congregations when we lead them – we can't lead them where we aren't able to go ourselves!

Some of the boxes commonly found in worship teams are: limited musical ability and ambition, fear of what people will think of us or what they say about us because we're up in front of them, our own need to be praised and thanked and made to feel special, our ego and need to feel important and significant, our previous experience or how our last worship team did things. Whatever the box is, for the sake of the people we serve, and for where God is leading us into, we need to get out from those limitations and walk in God's freedom, where God wants us to be and paid for us to be. That price was the highest that could be paid – the life of Jesus Christ, separation from heaven, and taking the punishment for our sins from us. Yet Jesus' victory over that death, punishment and separation means that we are now able to get out of any box freely.

Desire or obligation

Have you ever thought about what it is that motivates you to serve in church? I mean, really thought hard about it, looked into your heart, and given it serious consideration?

It should be the same as what motivates you to spend time with your friends and family because you love them, and spending time with them somehow makes you more complete. That's what relationship does, and was always God's plan for church, for it to be relationship-based, and for it to grow out of love and not obligation. Interestingly, the word 'religion' comes from the Latin word *religio*, which is influenced (according to the World Book Dictionary) by the verb *religare*, which means 'to bind', in the sense of 'place an obligation on'. Religion will only cause you to do things out of obligation, but relationship motivates from love.

Although our style of worship is not religious, in the traditional sense, and even though we preach freedom and relationship from our congregational pulpits, it doesn't stop religion seeping into our own walk with

God, and causing us to be defined and obligated by what we do. It happens without noticing, little by little, affecting over time our perspective and attitude, wearing away at our passion and vision, crumbling our relationships.

How do we stop this from happening? We keep the main thing the main thing – seek God first, pursue Him, be hungry for Him; love Him, love His people, love His house. Out of that comes the desire and motivation to serve no matter what circumstances or changes come our way, no matter what other people do or say. Living like that is living a worship life.

Deep calls unto deep

#hunger #David

Deep calls unto deep at the noise of Your waterfalls.
Psalm 42:7

Have you ever stood near a waterfall? Not one of those little trickles that wend their way down the side of a hill, glistening in the sunlight – but a high, wide waterfall that is constantly roaring as tonnes of water flow over it every minute. It is deafening, and overwhelming. David must have encountered one such waterfall to be able to express through this verse how his soul responded to God's outpouring of love in answer to his prayer. Something about standing before that waterfall must have reminded him of the raw, powerful and consuming sense of God's love.

This wasn't a shallow experience of God's presence, and it didn't come after just singing a few songs and being reminded of a few verses. It came after David stirred up within himself a hunger for God that overwhelmed his soul (verses 1-4). That hunger for God led him to worship and praise God passionately (verse 5), and then he experienced the closeness and realness of God's presence.

These verses challenge me to ask how hungry am I for God, and how hungry am I really willing to become. Not hungry to get an experience, but just hungry for God. How hungry are you for God? Have things settled into a nice comfortable way? Maybe it's time to start stirring up a greater hunger for God; not just hungry for His things, or His blessings, or His house, but just hungry for Him. All those other things come along with God, but they aren't what God wants us to be seeking.

Stir up a hunger for God, more than you've been before.

Armed with strength

It is God who arms me with strength, and makes my way perfect. He makes my feet like the feet of deer, and sets me on my high places. He teaches my hands to make war, so that my arms can bend a bow of bronze.
Psalm 18:32-34

These are great verses of encouragement and promise for us as worship leaders, as singers and musicians, serving God's house each week. When it's so easy to become settled into a way of doing things, and easily losing heart or focus when things go wrong or people say stuff that hurts, these verses remind us that our strength to serve God comes from God. He gives us what we need to serve Him and, if we let Him, He will train us and cause us to grow and do what we do better. When we do it in our own strength things quickly become wearying, samey, and religious. But in God's strength we find a lightness and ease in what we do, we find wisdom to do it, we find a fresh enthusiasm, we find things falling into place, and we find that we can do things we never thought we would.

So let's be honest with ourselves, and check where we're at. If you're finding things hard or wearisome, if you feel like you've lost the point or are just stuck in a rut, then it's not time to quit – rather take some time and seek God. Pray over these verses and let your faith grab hold of them. Ask God to forgive you for going off in your own strength and come back into His rest. Serving God, and serving His house and His people should never be a chore or a drain. Sure, there will always be some people that are hard to deal with, or situations that are awkward, but God has called us and made us to be His servants, His people. It's not a punishment, but a privilege, and God's promise is to enable us to do all that He's given us to do.

Keep seeking God

L ast time I looked at these verses:

> *It is God who arms me with strength, and makes my way*
> *perfect. He makes my feet like the feet of deer, and sets me*
> *on my high places. He teaches my hands to make war, so*
> *that my arms can bend a bow of bronze.*
> **Psalm 18:32-34**

Let's stick with them again.

This verses highlight three areas that we all face as we lead worship – the unknown (freshness in worship, God moving in ways that we haven't seen before), the high and unknown (worship that lifts us up to see from God's perspective, and to hear God's word), and the dangerous, high and unknown (coming against spiritual darkness, apathy and despair, strongholds of sin). This is where God leads us, but it is God that empowers and enables us to walk in them, to flourish in them, and to grow in understanding of them so we can teach, lead and empower others.

It all starts with seeking God. That should be our

highest priority in life, to seek and know Him. Everything we do flows out of our relationship with God. God wants to do amazing things through us. There are people's lives waiting to be touched, hearts waiting to be opened up to His love. Our cities are waiting on us to live for God.

Honour one another

Be devoted to one another in love. Honour one another above yourselves.
Romans 12:10, NIV

We've looked before at these and similar verses, as they sum up the culture of 'team' in Family Church. It's not about the job we're doing but who we're doing it with and who we're doing it for. God looks not for how well you play or sing but how you love and treat those you do life with. God's kingdom is built upon the values of love and selflessness, grace and serving. And even how well we play or sing will be motivated by love – a much stronger motivation than the desire to be a great musician or singer.

Let's keep growing in honouring each other – keep away from gossip, don't listen to negative talk; speak encouragement, show grace, cheer each other on. Let's continue to honour our leaders, the team leaders and our pastors – get behind their vision, don't let cynical or undermining talk flourish, but speak highly of them. Let's show honour to our congregations as we lead them, giving our very best to serve them (especially when it seems like they're not even slightly interested in engaging in worship!).

Honour reveals the value we feel for something or someone. In honouring each other we recognise the value that God has placed on each individual life, and it becomes part of our worship life.

Servant-minded or servant-hearted?

#serving #servantheart #mindset

There's a big difference between being servant-minded and servant hearted.

If you're thinking just about the job you're doing, getting that done right, making sure all that you've been asked to do is done, then you might be only servant-minded, and not servant hearted.

If you care about the recognition you get for something you've done, or get upset if you're not given the credit for it (and especially if the credit goes to someone else) then you may be servant-minded and not servant-hearted.

If you've found a degree of time sacrifice that you're comfortable with (or maybe slightly uncomfortable because it's a little more than you really wanted to sacrifice, but you'll live with it) then you're probably servant-minded and not servant-hearted.

If "that's someone else's problem" or "I don't really do that, I really feel I should serve within my giftings and calling", or "Well, if they understood my problems a bit more, and what I have to give up and go through just to make this happen, they might change what they do and help me out a bit more!", then it's pretty likely you're servant-minded, not servant-hearted.

Jesus talks about the servant-minded and the servant-hearted in John:

> *I am the good shepherd. The good shepherd gives His life for the sheep. But a hireling, he who is not the shepherd, one who does not own the sheep, sees the wolf coming and leaves the sheep and flees; and the wolf catches the sheep and scatters them. The hireling flees because he is a hireling and does not care about the sheep. I am the good shepherd; and I know My sheep, and am known by My own. As the Father knows Me, even so I know the Father; and I lay down My life for the sheep. And other sheep I have which are not of this fold; them also I must bring, and they will hear My voice; and there will be one flock and one shepherd.*
> ***John 10:11-16***

The hireling, or servant-minded, is there to do a job, does the job, goes home at the end of the job – but if that job suffers difficulty or threat, then he or she is off.

Jesus, our example of servant-hearted, is there not because of the job but because of the 'sheep'.

Servant-hearted people care. Care comes from the heart, not the mind. The life of a servant-hearted person is defined by the love and care that comes from their heart. For them it's not about the job but about who it is all for – for them it's not even a job, it's who they are and they do it because they care. Jesus say that we are known as His not by our knowledge of the Bible, or attendance at events, or by how spiritual our current Facebook status is, but by our love for each other. Loving each other comes from being servant-hearted, not servant-minded.

A good report

Over the last few weeks I've been focusing these messages on different aspects of our team culture. A podcast from the Life Church Worship Team, Bradford, had some good teaching on building team, and one of their principles is on the power of a good and bad report.

In Numbers 13, spies are sent into the Promised Land, and they return with fruit they've found and a report of what's ahead. Two spies – Caleb and Joshua – give a good report, but the other ten spies give a bad report. That bad report spreads like wildfire throughout the nation – around 6 million people – and by the end of the day the whole nation is in uproar against Moses for leading them out of captivity into apparent certain death. That bad report stops a whole generation from entering into their Promised Land. The idea of walking into an already-populated country and taking it over must have seemed quite strange, at the very least, suicidal at worst. But then, they'd just walked through an ocean on dry land and seen an entire army drown, all for the sake of their rescue and journey into God's promise.

It is amazing the damage a bad report can do, and how quickly it can do it! Had the nation of Israel chosen to believe God's promise and follow Moses and their leaders into the Promised Land, there wouldn't have been a forty-year wait, disappointment and disillusionment. Even those who believed the good report had to live with the consequences of others believing the bad report.

In our teams we must always be careful to avoid the bad report. We must not just speak a good report, we must LIVE a good report. People see our lives, as well as hear our words, and a life lived unfaithfully will give a bad report regardless of the good words spoken. Live a life that displays the good report that the songs we lead convey. Let others see that what we sing on stage, we live out off stage. Even when things happen that we may think strange or unachievable, let's keep the good report on our lips and in our hearts. Speak well of our leaders, speak well of each other; but not only that, let everyone else see that that is what you believe by the way you live, and not just words.

A healthy team grows from a good report:

Good news (report) makes for good health.
Proverbs 15:3 (NLT)

Think big!

#GodsWord #revelation

In Exodus 33, Moses has a conversation with God about the way ahead for the nation of Israel. Moses is trying to understand what God wants, but his limited thinking is stopping him from seeing what God's plans are. Moses feels like God has missed off part of the plan (verse 12: "You haven't let me know who You will send with me" – who's going to help me, I need more resources, it can't work like this!), but he has the sense to ask God that His presence always go with them – in fact, Moses knows that without God, they're just another nation, with nothing to set the apart from the rest. Moses now knows that God is with him, but he still is struggling to see it happening, so he asks God, "Show me Your glory". This leads to God hiding Moses in a cleft of a rock, covering him with His hand while He passes by, and then lifting the hand enough for Moses to see His back as He passes by. What a mind-blowing experience for Moses. All of a sudden he sees God in all His strength revealed, his mind explodes with the understanding of just how immense and powerful

God is. His thinking is never the same – how can it be?

What follows that experience is the moment when God hands to Moses the Ten Commandments, with chapters of law regarding how the nation of Israel should live, how the tabernacle should be built, how God should be worshipped – words that go into incredible detail about how God wants the nation of Israel to be.

The thing is, if God had given Moses those laws BEFORE his cleft-of-the-rock experience, it would have just remained law. Those words would have settled in Moses struggling, small-thinking mind-set and would then have been imposed on Israel without any understanding of what it all meant. AFTER that experience, Moses' thinking is so enlarged that these laws become more than just law, and he is able to speak them to a nation of around 6 million people and in one day change the culture of that nation. Literally, they become a new nation through God's Word to Moses, defined by God's thoughts and God's heart, rather than law. Those words have the power to change the lifestyle of a nation all because the mind that received them had been enlarged to carry those words and keep them as words of life. Without that enlarged thinking those words would have been like death to the nation of Israel.

How powerful, and essential, is big thinking for us as leaders, eh? God is leading us as a church, and as congregations, into growth, new things, different things. When God's Word comes, if our thinking isn't big then those words will become a law to us – not life-giving but constrictive and hard. With big thinking – thinking that has been enlarged through seeing God rather than ourselves or our circumstances – then those words bring life. Sure they bring challenge, change and a little insecurity, but only to lead us into God's good plan for us.

There's a whole new year ahead of us, with so much that God has prepared for us to do. We NEED to think bigger, see beyond our limitations to God's strength and power. Because change is coming, bigger challenges are coming, and when it comes it will either bring life or death (not literal death!) to us depending on our thinking.

Let's not settle for where we are now. Let's keep looking up, looking to God, and enlarging our thinking so we can receive God's Word and run with it.

Christ-centred

Christ is the centre of all creation, of all that we are, of all that's been and is to come. For us in the worship team, it's not a case of "Oh, let's make this all about Jesus" but of realising that Jesus always has been and always will be at the centre of all things and so we must put aside everything else – our own ideas, plans, thoughts, styles, experience, knowledge – so that we uncover and reveal Christ. Being Christ-centred means losing completely all of our previous motivations, and finding that Jesus is the very beginning of what we do and why we do it.

Rather than go looking for where we can add Jesus to what we do, we need to stop what we're doing, throw off our own ideas and creations until we find that all that remains is Jesus, and then start from there, start from Him and let everything we do come from the relationship and revelation of Jesus Christ.

We allow Christ to become off-centre in our lives when we let our own desires, ambitions, ideas and plans take over – even the ones that are actually alright and could produce success and growth. To get back to being Christ-centred we need to let go of all those things, let them drop off like rags and find the source of all we are in Christ, and Him alone.

Your singing, your musicianship, your serving in church – find Christ at the centre of it so that the life of Christ flows out through it.

Commissioned

#commission #calling #values

The worship team never has been, and never will be, just a group of people who enjoy singing or playing and have somehow wound up doing it together in the first part of a church service (in some churches it feels like that's what's going on, though!). We have a calling that goes way beyond the songs we sing and play.

We are commissioned by God to carry His presence to His people. That isn't just a nice, spiritually-sounding phrase but a calling to live lives that draw people to God, not turn them away; to be responsive to the leading of the Holy Spirit in our everyday lives, and help people to turn their eyes onto Jesus. Strong character, not great talent, carries the presence of God.

God commissions us to carry His people into His presence, by creating an atmosphere that excites the inner man to burst out in praise and worship. By daring to be extravagant in our own worship. By daring to imagine new songs, anthems, sounds and rhythms. The soul and spirit is stirred by creativity and passion.

You may have come into the worship team 'by accident' or because a friend brought you, or because you wanted use your gift in some way. But your involvement now you're in doesn't come from your own plans, but from God's calling on you to serve Him and His house. Realise now that you are a commissioned worship team member, called and led by God's purpose, not your own. Understand the responsibility that comes with that commission, and take it on wholeheartedly. When you do something because you know you're called to it, that understanding changes the way you do that thing. You don't treat it so lightly anymore; you find yourself thinking how could you do your part better, how could you help others do their part better.

Let's keep reminding ourselves of our commission in the worship team: to carry God's presence to His people, and to carry God's people into His presence, through character and creativity. This is your calling.

iscipled

#discipleship #values

At Family Church we value discipleship – the daily decision to walk out the life God has called us to and is leading us through. Discipleship is marked by a life that is fruitful, regardless of the season through which it is going:

> *Happy are those who don't listen to the wicked, who don't go where sinners go, who don't do what evil people do. They love the Lord's teachings, and they think about those teachings day and night. They are strong, like a tree planted by a river. The tree produces fruit in season, and its leaves don't die. Everything they do will succeed.*
> **Psalms 1:1-3, NCV**

Discipleship submits to and responds well to correction:

> *People who accept discipline are on the pathway to life, but those who ignore correction will go astray.*
> **Proverbs 10:17, NLT**

Discipleship results in consistent growth, and the falling away of immature and poor attitudes:

When I was a child, I spoke and thought and reasoned as
a child. But when I grew up, I put away childish things.
1 Corinthians 13:11, NLT

As leaders of worship, leading the church into God's presence not just through weekly congregational meetings but step by step further into all that God is leading the church as it grows, we need to keep ourselves submitted to leadership and to God's inner voice. The fruit of our worship discipleship is a church and community that experience and engage with God's miraculous, bondage-breaking, healing, restorative, grace-filled presence. Discipleship is a choice, but once we choose it we are in God's hands to be moulded, refined and crafted into His workmanship. We are called to be carriers – of His presence and of His people. Discipleship enables us to carry more and more.

ible-believing

#GodsWord #values

My son, give attention to my words; incline your ear to my sayings. Do not let them depart from your eyes; keep them in the midst of your heart; for they are life to those who find them, and health to all their flesh. Keep your heart with all diligence, for out of it spring the issues of life.
Proverbs 4:20-23

The Bible, and the truth that it contains, is the very foundation of our faith, and without it we have nothing. There is more in the Bible than we could hope to discover in a lifetime, but it is the pursuit of truth that God calls us to each day – to not let His words be reduced to print or pixels but to seek Him in it daily. Those verses above, from Proverbs, say that God's words are life to those that find it. We must be ever seeking, questing, journeying to know Him more through the words that have been handed down to us through the centuries. We read not to satisfy a sense of religious duty or put a tick in a box, but because these words bring life – God's life – into our worlds.

Let's pursue the word of God with the same thirst that David wrote about – "my soul thirst for you, in a dry and thirsty land where there is no water". That's an overwhelming thirst, an uncomfortable thirst. But we have the promise that our thirst will be quenched, when we seek God, to know Him and to know His word.

We believe the Bible, because it is the Word of Life – Jesus revealed to us. We need to know the Bible more, so we can know Jesus more.

Community

Community is at the very heart of God's plan for humanity – we were made to live in community, to be part of a family, not independent or alone. Community is established through common values and vision, and is bound through relationship. Our relationships with each other model God's relationship with us – based on how we choose to be, not what others have done, enabled and empowered through grace and love.

Community is essential for us as a worship team, because the strength of our leading flows out of the strength of our community – otherwise it's just performance, a job that we turn up and do. Church – life, even – is more than just the jobs we do. It's all about people. We all come broken. We all need each other. We can never let the songs or the style take precedence over the most important part of this design of God for His people – the people themselves.

We serve the community of people that we are as much part of as anyone else. The way to make that work is to follow what the Bible says: honour each other, love another, prefer others above yourself, forgive, encourage, bless, comfort. God isn't actually looking for us to become a great worship team, He's looking for us to love each other. We become a great worship team not when we develop our musicianship or singing to a high degree of excellence but when we walk in love.

> *Behold, how good and how pleasant it is for brethren to dwell together in unity! It is like the precious oil upon the head, running down on the beard, the beard of Aaron, running down on the edge of his garments. It is like the dew of Hermon, descending upon the mountains of Zion; for there the Lord commanded the blessing – life forevermore.*
> **Psalms 133:1-3**

Community is the heart of God's kingdom, more important than any song or riff. The world needs the refreshing and blessing that comes upon the church that walks in community.

Spiritual

We are a spiritual team, not just a natural musical team. In fact, the natural aspect of what we do has no real effect if the spiritual aspect is left out, ignored, overlooked or placed second. Everything we do flows out of the spiritual part of our lives.

God made us body, soul and spirit. All three parts are important but if we are to live in all that God has called and purposes to, the spiritual part of our lives has to be the directional part. Yet, more often than not it is the soulish part of our lives that are lead by and respond to – especially creative people. Our souls are designed to be creative, to be imaginative and passionate, to find beauty and aspire to create it. But when we are led by our souls we become self-focused and egotistical, over-sensitive and unteachable. For creativity to be life giving it must find its source in our spirit, our inner man that has been made alive in Christ. Jesus Christ is the original Creator, and for us to find purpose and influence in our creativity we must be found in Christ, not in ourselves.

Being a spiritual people also means that we need

the Holy Spirit in all that we do. We wage a spiritual war, not a natural one. Our strength comes from our spiritual life, not our ability or knowledge, or even how good we think we are. We lead people in a spiritual act, not jut the natural acts of singing, clapping and dancing. Worship is the breath of our spiritual life, and our calling is to be leaders in it in God's house. A life lived soulishly, or even carnally, will quickly become empty and shallow when trying to engage in the spiritual act of worship.

Being spiritual people, and growing as spiritual people, means going deeper with God. We can lead God's people to a deeper place of corporate worship when we choose to go deeper with God ourselves – not waiting for someone else to tell us, or for when it feels right, but because we long to know God more.

Your spiritual life is vital – give it the highest priority in your life.

Relevance

For us as a worship team, relevance goes way further than just using the latest songs or having a sound that echoes that of the current charts, or having a stage that looks modern, funky and atmospheric, or having all the main instruments that ideally should be in a band.

Our role, our primary function, as a team is to point people to Jesus, and Jesus was and is the most relevant person on the earth. To be relevant means to be connected to or relating to the matter in hand, what's happening in life at this moment. Life itself comes from God, so no one is more relevant to life than the Author of life Himself.

Our relevancy as a team and as a ministry comes from how central to, and how focused upon, Jesus it is. To be relevant to the church, the worship we lead must carry the fragrance of God's presence, that fragrance that draws people out of their self-focusedness to lift and fix their eyes on Jesus, who is their Provider, Healer, Restorer, Protector, Guide, all that they need. What we do has relevance when it draws people to

God who is more real than their circumstances, who sits above our problems and walks with us in them. Who or what could be more connected to what we, and everyone who comes to our congregations on a Sunday, and everyone we come into contact with during the week, than Jesus. And it is Jesus that people should meet through the worship we lead, not just us and the songs we play and sing.

The natural tools we use to reach out to people are useful, but they won't last – they change over the years. We can use them but we can't rely on them or consider anything built with them to last for long. If we want what we do as a worship team to be enduring and have eternal impact, then there is only one ingredient we can 'use' and rely on, and that is Jesus Himself, His presence and truth. As long as we keep Jesus at the centre of all we do, we can be stripped of every natural tool and still be entirely relevant.

Responsive

There are many ways that we can be responsive as a worship team.

First and foremost, we must be spiritually responsive to God's voice – we must be listening to Him, have our ear tuned to His direction (and away from our own soulish ambition or opinion). We must be ready to respond to Him when He stirs something new in us. We must be ready to respond when He calls us back after we've wandered away in our own strength, or when He corrects an attitude or wayward thought. A responsive heart toward God is the foundation for being a leader. Our experience, knowledge and skill – no matter what level – will not enable us to 'walk upon the water', when God calls to us to do something we've never done before; only an open, ready and responsive heart will get us to step out of the boat.

We need to be responsive to our leaders – this is practical as well as spiritual, as leaders provide the spiritual covering and authority for a team, and being unresponsive to a leader pretty much puts you on the outside of that team. When we're leading worship, the worship leader needs a responsive team behind them, ready to change the direction or dynamic of a song at a moment's notice. To be responsive like that requires preparation on our part, learning and understanding the songs we use as well as listening and learning to follow the worship leader. When our leaders send out a challenge, our response should be to step up and take on that challenge. If something happens that you don't like, how do you respond? Do you moan about or berate the leader (bad response) or do you approach and chat over the situation to reach a positive conclusion (good response)? Words are easy – it's in our actions that our true response is shown.

We also need to be responsive to each other. We've said many times before that the strength of our teams is built on good relationships. Do we respond with grace and humility to each other? If we find ourselves in a difficult situation where things are going wrong or taking time to be dealt with, do we respond with patience or kick off? If we hear criticism or rumours, is our response to protect our team or to allow those negative words to continue? To respond in every situation with grace is a choice, because it's far easier to respond with a sense of retribution or judgment. Things happen, people have off days (or are just generally off!), situations change – how we respond determines how strong our commitment to each other is, because a good response in difficult circumstances requires real faith and persistence and a determination to live by God's kingdom principles, no matter how hard. Again, words are easy, but actions reveal the true heart of responsiveness.

Responsiveness is a heart issue, not based on a formula or rule book. You can't follow a laid-down guide to how you should respond – it comes from a heart that is set on God's ways, set on seeking Him and serving His people.

Pot-plant or Planted?

Those who are planted in the house of the Lord shall flourish in the courts of our God.
Psalms 92:13

Worship is about how we live our lives, and when we serve in God's house, that serving comes from the outflow of worship in our lives. We flourish in serving God's purposes only when we are planted in His house, because the church is God's answer to the hurt and searching of this world. The church is the answer. We are the answer. Us!

We can't do this by ourselves – God has designed it to be this way, because the church is a community and family built on love, reflecting the community and family of the Trinity. To receive the benefits of being in community, as well as to be able to serve it well, we need to be planted in, rooted deeply in.

So are you planted in this house, or are you just a pot-plant? What's the difference – well, we know what it's like to be planted; a pot-plant, on the other hand, has no purpose except to provide some decoration!

It isn't part of the fibre of the house, its roots are not connected to the roots of the house, it isn't drawing its nourishment and food from the house but is constantly demanding its own food. You can tell if someone is a pot-plant by how they treat church – the people, the commitments, the values. If a person's own values, opinions and interests are more important, you know they aren't planted in the soil of the house but in their own little container. If all they ever talk about is themselves, or what they've done, then you know they are a pot-plant in their own world, serving their own purpose.

When you become planted in the soil of God's house, you will grow more than you ever could before, the fruit you bear is healthier, and your foundation is stronger. When you are planted you become part of the bigger picture of God's house and it stops being about you. People who are planted are very hard to move or be shaken. Pot-plants come and go, and leave no mark on the house.

For God's life to flow through us we need to be planted into the soil of God's house where His life can flow into us. Be planted, not a pot-plant!

enerous

Six days before the Passover Feast, Jesus went to Bethany, where Lazarus lived. (Lazarus is the man Jesus raised from the dead.) There they had a dinner for Jesus. Martha served the food, and Lazarus was one of the people eating with Jesus. Mary brought in a pint of very expensive perfume made from pure nard. She poured the perfume on Jesus' feet, and then she wiped his feet with her hair. And the sweet smell from the perfume filled the whole house. Judas Iscariot, one of Jesus' followers who would later turn against him, was there. Judas said, "This perfume was worth an entire year's wages. Why wasn't it sold and the money given to the poor?" But Judas did not really care about the poor; he said this because he was a thief. He was the one who kept the moneybox, and he often stole from it. Jesus answered, "Leave her alone. It was right for her to save this perfume for today, the day for me to be prepared for burial. You will always have the poor with you, but you will not always have me."
John 12:1-8, NCV

This is one of the most well-known examples in the Bible of generosity in worship. Mary bought a bottle of perfume that was worth an entire year's wages (so we're not talking about the aftershave counter at the local convenience store here – nowadays you'd have to go to somewhere like Harrods to buy the equivalent!), and in the space of a few minutes poured the entire bottle over Jesus feet. Now, as it was then, the thought of doing something similar would, for especially religious people, raise a cry of, "That could have been spent on something far more profitable for society". You see here the two opposing forces that inspire worship – extravagant generosity, and meanness. Interestingly, the meanness always has a facade of generosity to it, and gives the impression of spirituality. But there is something about real heart-felt generosity, unrestrained giving, in worship that identifies it as real – it has a beautiful smell, you can see that a sacrifice has been made but it's not about the sacrifice but about the One to whom the sacrifice is made.

Living a worship life, there should be a selfless generosity to all that we do. We could never out-give God, as Pastor Andy often says – a worship life has no limits, doesn't see limits, and doesn't put limits on others. To grow as worshippers, and as worship leaders, we need to be generous with what we have right now.

The generous soul will be made rich, and he who waters will also be watered himself.
Proverbs 11:25

Connecting

Last Sunday Pastor Andy spoke about us being in a time of strengthening – before we start to stretch again, and in our last Core & General Leaders meeting we talked about what 'strength' looks like for our teams. One of the strengths mentioned was being able to connect with God and with the congregation, and that is something that we have been working on and developing in band for a while now.

Connecting with God means being authentic in our worship, keeping Him as the reason and centre of all that we do, bringing our very best as an offering of devotion and love to Him. Connecting with the congregation has two 'areas of application' – on and off the stage. We lead from a stage – the stage is the focus and place of leadership for our meetings, and we need to be selfless when we are standing and serving on it, not allowing personal agendas or a need for attention to motivate us but a desire to serve and carry the church through passionate worship. On the stage we demonstrate worship but we don't zone out into a personal worship zone – we invite the congregation into a united expression of worship. We smile, we move, we jump, we raise our hands, we open our eyes, we open ourselves up, we give of who we are to the church – all to create an atmosphere that empowers and release the church to worship freely.

Off stage we need to continue that openness and friendliness, engaging in conversation (especially with new people), saying hello as we pass people in the corridor, not hiding away or keeping to ourselves. We are leaders on AND off the stage, it doesn't end when we put down the microphone, unplug the guitar or turn off the keyboard.

God isn't fragile

In some Pentecostal or charismatic circles of church so much emphasis is placed on not offending the Holy Spirit, that if we should put a foot wrong His presence would leave a meeting, the glory would end, the miracles would disappear; I think that creates a misunderstanding of God's presence, that it is so fragile that the smallest thing would cause the Holy Spirit to bolt, almost as if God doesn't really want to manifest His presence and His power on and through us and is looking for a reason not to be there! Maybe I'm overplaying it, but I have known many Christians who have desired God more out of fear that He might leave if they didn't, than any kind of faith based on His promise and His word.

2 Corinthians 4:7 says that "we have this treasure in earthen vessels", that it is us that is fragile, not the treasure of God's presence in our lives. God has promised over and over again that he would be with us, that He would never leave us. He knows that we are broken, fragile people, working our way through a process of restoration and healing as we grow to

know Him more. He knows are failings and our weaknesses just as much as our strengths and talents. And yet He chooses to fill our lives with His presence. He chooses to live with our inconsistencies. He chooses to use and work through us, even though we mess up.

As a team called to carry God's presence we should have faith in His promises that He will be with us, He will work through us, He will lead us and He will empower and equip us. He has chosen to do it through us – He's chosen us to do it through. By walking in humility and submission, by being selfless and showing grace and love, we experience the incredible blessing of God's power working through us. A heart that is submitted to God will change, because that is what God promised to do. When we lead, we lead by faith in the promises of God – that He wants to reveal Himself to and through His people; that He wants to heal and restore; that He wants to commission and send out – all from a place of worship.

David's model of leadership

#leadership #integrity #skill

*He also chose David His servant, and took him from the
sheepfolds; from following the ewes that had young He brought
him, to shepherd Jacob His people, and Israel His inheritance.
So he [David] shepherded them according to the integrity of
His heart, and guided them by the skillfulness of his hands.*
Psalm 78:70

God chose David and took him out of relative
obscurity, giving him responsibility for the
whole nation of Israel. That last verse shows of David
handled the burden he'd been given – having a heart
passionate and honest towards God, and training
his natural abilities as best he could. He led the nation
of Israel through character and creativity. And even
though he made some major errors, God still saw
him as having a heart after His own, and honoured him
long after he passed away. When Solomon took over
as king the one thing he asked God for – and God
would have given him anything – was wisdom so that
he could lead the people of Israel well. He understood

the burden of leading people and knew that he needed more than he had in himself to do it.

We also are called and chosen to lead people, and with that calling comes God's burden for His people – love, mercy and purpose. Without God's help we will revert to rules and ceremony to help us carry that burden – same if our heart is not humbled, submitted and passionate for Him. Without love, mercy and purpose we rely on people to meet our needs, get frustrated when they don't, and become disheartened when it gets hard. But through David's model of character and creativity, we find that God is able to incredible things through limited resources; we see potential and opportunity, rather than lack or brick wall, because our eyes are on God and not on ourselves.

$\mathcal{A}$ thick skin?

#grace #community #family #purpose

You hear often the phrase "Oh, you need to develop a thick skin" in all kinds of places – all places generally that involve working with other people. The world would say that to get along you have to build a bigger and better barrier around yourself. You even hear it sometimes in some church situations, especially if you want to become a leader. Actually, it's not a 'thick skin' that's going to protect you, or enable you to work with 'interesting' people, but a greater understanding of grace.

Grace is what we all walk in, day by day – the knowledge that all that we've done wrong has been erased by the sacrifice made by Jesus on the cross, and the sin gap that stood between us and God has been forever and permanently bridged; and the endowment of heaven's power and wisdom to walk in this world differently, carrying God's kingdom everywhere we go. And this grace is everyone's, which means it's just as much freely available to that 'interesting' person we mentioned earlier as it is to you – neither deserved it and neither will be refused it.

Grace is what enables us to live as a family, as a community. It is what enables us to work and serve so closely together and not be riled, angered or turned off by what we see when we look into each other's lives. Grace has covered us all and grace qualifies us all. Grace is more than overlooking the differences or offenses – it is God's gift of His presence and power to us that makes us His people, light to this dark world. We are family, and we grow only because of grace. If we lose sight of grace, we lose sight of our purpose.

$\mathcal{S}$urrender

#surrender #faith #believe

To raise our arms and hands in worship is not just 'what we do' at our kind of church, it is representative of our surrender to God, acknowledging Him as greater, higher, bigger, able. It's us saying, "Actually, I can't do it, and I know it. I'm just going to let you instead". In and of itself, raising hands is just an act, but combined with the words that we are singing at the time, words that have engaged and connected with our heart and not just our minds, it makes a powerful statement to the world and the enemy, and becomes a powerful tool for the building of God's kingdom in our world, and a powerful weapon against the warring in our minds and emotions. It may be nerves that hold us back, or hurt, or doubt, or a sense of guilt – but when we 'give in' to God, and bring to Him our heart-felt worship, lifting our hands in surrender and adoration, all of these things are blown out of the way, they're literally disintegrated by the overwhelming knowledge of God's love that He pours into us. Surrendering to God in worship opens the doors to God's heavenly creative power to turn around desperate and impossible situations, to overturn charges thrown against us, to change things that we in ourselves would have no hope of changing.

The first line of the chorus of the Chris Tomlin song we're learning (and it's title) is "I lift my hands to believe again". To believe God's word means surrendering our own will and plan; it means saying "This makes no sense, I don't know how it'll work, I'm not even sure it will – but I surrender to You and Your purpose, I choose to trust You over my own knowledge and experience." That's powerful worship.

Surrender is our first choice

Though there may be moments where we deliberately choose to surrender, it is actually something that must be lived out, that must be in the core of our personal culture and mindset to life.

Elizabeth Elliot, the wife of Ecuadorian missionary Jim Elliot, wrote once that surrender is not something you do in an instant – something that is lifelong takes a lifetime to surrender. In other words, surrender is something that happens every day of your life, not just at a special moment during a church meeting.

The founder of the Salvation Army, William Booth, understood that the degree of God's greatness and power in his life came from the degree of his surrender.

And Oswald Chambers, the early 20th-century preacher, wrote that, for us to fully carry the strain and burden of God's kingdom purposes, we have to come to the place where, through the refining fire of a relationship with Jesus Christ, our only heart's cry is to be used and sent wherever God may ask, doing whatever He asks and not what we have ambition for; just as Isaiah prayed after he had been refined in God's presence, "here I am, Lord, send me."

Sometimes God lets us pursue a course in our own strength so that we can more quickly come to the place of realisation that we can't do it, and surrender to Him. At that point we change the foundation of our decision making, through the act of repentance, so that our first choice now is always to serve in His strength and not to try in our own.

Authority through surrender

#surrender #authority

Then the king said to Ittai the Gittite, "Why are you also going with us? Return and remain with the king. For you area foreigner and also an exile from your own place. In fact, you came only yesterday. Should I make you wander up and down with us today, since I go I know not where? Return, and take your brethren back. Mercy and truth be with you." But Ittai answered the king and said, "As the Lord lives, and as my lord the king lives, surely in whatever place my lord the king shall be, whether in death or life, even there also your servant will be." So David said to Ittai, "Go, and cross over." Then Ittai the Gittite and all his men and all the little ones who were with him crossed over.
2 Samuel 15:19-22

David was getting out of Jerusalem as Absalom made his move to try and take over. As they were going David noticed the king of another country leaving with him, and says, "No, you go home". Ittai wasn't an Israelite, wasn't part of David's court. He'd literally shown up the day before. He didn't come to show aggression or attempt warfare. Ittai chose to surrender himself to David, which meant handing over the rulership of his kingdom, his armies, his wealth and resource, to David. Then three chapters later, this:

> *And David numbered the people who were with him, and set captains of thousands and captains of hundreds over them. Then David sent out one third of the people under the hand of Joab, one third under the hand of Abishai the son of Zeruiah, Joab's brother, and one third under the hand of Ittai the Gittite. And the king said to the people, "I also will surely go out with you myself."*
> **2 Samuel 18:1-3**

Ittai's surrender to David brought him to a place of authority. He went from being the king of a foreign nation to being commander over a third of David's army!

Our authority comes from a place of surrender. It doesn't come from our skill, or experience, or recommendation from others. When we surrender to God, He raises us up – He positions us with His authority. Absalom tried to take authority, through subtlety and manipulation, through his own effort. You can't sustain any authority gained through selfish ambition. Ittai was given authority through his surrender and devotion.

*T*he answer is surrender

L et's look at these verses from two classic hymns:

O to grace how great a debtor
Daily I'm constrained to be!
Let Thy goodness, like a fetter,
Bind my wandering heart to Thee.
Prone to wander, Lord, I feel it,
Prone to leave the God I love;
Here's my heart, O take and seal it,
Seal it for Thy courts above.[5]

Robinson understood the human nature: without God's grace we are 'prone to wander' – and the answer is surrender. He describes eloquently how, when we do surrender ourselves daily, we find this incredible connection to the courts of heaven, to God's presence. In surrender we not only find the answer to our unfaithfulness, in being bound by God's goodness to His own heart, we find ourselves before His throne, in intimacy with Him, encountering His presence

---

5   *Come thou font of every blessing*, Robert Robinson, 1757. Public domain.

and glory, His power and love.
The second hymn describes this too:

All to Jesus I surrender,
Lord, I give myself to thee,
Fill me with thy love and power,
Let thy blessing fall on me.
All to Jesus I surrender;
Now I feel the sacred flame.
Oh, the joy of full salvation!
Glory, glory, to his name![6]

In surrender we encounter the flame of His salvation,
and experience an outpouring of worship and adoration.
DeVenter said this of writing the words of the
hymn *I Surrender All*:

"For some time, I had struggled between developing my
talents in the field of art and going into full-time evangelistic
work. At last the pivotal hour of my life came, and I
surrendered all. A new day was ushered into my life. I
became an evangelist and discovered down deep in my
soul a talent hitherto unknown to me. God had hidden a
song in my heart, and touching a tender chord, He caused
me to sing."[7]

---

6   *I surrender all*, Judson W. Van DeVenter, 1896. Public domain.

7   *101 More Hymn Stories*, Kenneth W. Osbeck (Kregel Publications, 1985, p136; available on http://books.
google.com)

DeVentner loved the arts and his soul's desire was to pursue that field using his talents, but in the end he surrendered his life to pursue the calling of God. When he did, though, he found a God had released him into using his talent but for much higher purpose. His connection to the courts of God, through surrender, turned his soulish desire into a selfless kingdom purpose.

The right way to carry

#surrender #carry #need #rest #burden

If you are tired from carrying heavy burdens, come to me and I will give you rest. Take the yoke I give you. Put it on your shoulders and learn from me. I am gentle and humble, and you will find rest. This yoke is easy to bear, and this burden is light.
Matthew 11:28-30 (CEV)

We all can easily find ourselves carrying multiple 'burdens' or 'loads'. The word Jesus uses here refers to carrying something 'to the point of exhaustion' – ie. we just accept it, we don't change it, and we keep going until we cannot go any further. We are called to be carriers – carriers of His presence, and carriers of His people – but this is not meant to be a burden that brings us to our knees in exhaustion. Jesus said that His burden would not cause that to happen.

So what is it that we're carrying that gets us so tired? Usually it is the desires and priorities of our soul that cause us to be weighed down. It is our need for personal musical excellence, our need for recognition, our need for the job to be done, our need to show ourselves faithful, our need to be right, our need to be in control. These things, some of them anyway, aren't bad at all, but without care they will all wear us out.

We are supposed to carry things, but Jesus calls us to surrender our own burdens and take His. We are still doing 'the work' but we find His rest in all that we do. To carry Jesus' burden means to surrender ours. Carrying His presence and carrying His people should be, as Jesus says, easy and light. If we find that we are becoming exhausted or weighed down – in our hearts and souls – we need to re-examine what we are really carrying, and make sure we surrender any self-appointed burden to Jesus, and accept back His burden instead.

Continuous grace

There is a high expectation and demand when joining the worship team, and we make no apologies for that, because we believe in the power of heaven that is upon what we do. We've been given great responsibility, by our leaders and by God, to lead and to carry God's people, to inspire and guide them, to stir them up and love them through, to bring encouragement and boldness in faith and to bring comfort and truth in hurt; all through the songs we play and sing! But then we're not just playing and singing songs – we're bringing what God has put in us to His people and allowing God to use it to bring His healing, comfort, strength, revelation, peace, joy, understanding, and so much more, into this world. It's really a small part we play, in the grand scheme of things, but it is a part that we must give ourselves wholeheartedly to – doing so is our own expression of love and worship.

We're all at different places and stages in life, and skill, but that doesn't change the demand placed on us. Yet in the midst of that demand is God's promise, that we can come before Him, right to His throne, and receive the grace we need to accomplish all He's called us to do (Hebrews 4:16). Though the demand is great, the grace to serve is even greater, more than we could imagine. We're not meant to be able to manage it all in our own strength. A vision or dream that you can accomplish yourself is most likely not from God, because He looks for us to use faith – and no faith is needed to do something you know you can do. The promise in this verse from Hebrews has no time limit or proviso linked to it: whenever we need help – WHENEVER – we can receive God's abundant grace and mercy. Let's keep building our team – and your part in it – on God's grace, and not ability or experience, nor allow it to be defined by the past.

Authenticity

One of the things that makes us who we are is the authenticity of our worship – we believe that worship has to be real, has to come from a heart that is devoted to God, has to be honest and real and faith-filled. Authenticity empowers our leading when we stand before our congregation, no matter what its size and no matter how many of us there are on a team. Without authenticity in our own worship, what gets brought to the church each week is shallow and over-dependent on performance. With authenticity our 'performance' becomes a part of our worship, a desire to do the very best because we love God and we love our church. Jesus said, in John 4:23-24, that God looks for people with truth in their worship – authenticity, honesty, faith.

When Paul and Silas were locked up in prison, their worship was authentic, because it wasn't based on their horrific circumstances but their faith and relationship with God. When the woman broke the jar of perfume over Jesus' feet, her worship was authentic because it wasn't based on show ("Hey, look at me, look at how much I love Jesus!") but on her deep gratitude, knowing that the change in her life came about through undeserved grace. In the midst of being stoned to death, Stephen worshipped God authentically, not because he was trying to make his killers feel guilty or to annoy them but because right there he saw God and his revelation of God overwhelmed his pain, humiliation and fear.

Authenticity doesn't come because of the situation but because of your revelation of God and your relationship with Him. Keep pursuing and desiring God!

Godly passion

There was a time, early in my Christian faith walk, that I thought that being passionate for God meant throwing aside every other passion in my life, so that He was my only passion. I've learnt since that God isn't asking for us to do that. We're made to be passionate about stuff, even stuff that has no eternal significance whatsoever.

We're uniquely and individually made, and it's our passions – the things we value and enjoy – that define who we are. Proverbs 4:23 says, "Keep your heart with all diligence, for out of it spring the issues of life". In the NIV the second half of that verse is "For everything you do flows from [your heart]". Everything about us – what we do, what we choose, what we value, what we love, what we hate, what we fear – flows from our heart. We are so wonderfully and intricately made, by God, to value many things. But none of those need be thrown away in an attempt to demonstrate a passion for God.

Our passion for God must be foremost in our lives, and we must allow that godly passion to inform, influence and inspire all our other passions. When we do that we find God's purpose in our design, in our makeup. Some passions fall away because they're clearly not right for us. Some passions find new purpose, new direction – suddenly we see how God could use us to influence a part of our world that we thought we just did as a hobby! Some new passions are birthed in us, as we sense God's heart for parts of our world that He wants us to think and act differently about.

Carrying dynamite

#dynamite #power #GodsSpirit #Pentecost #devotion

But when the Holy Spirit comes to you, you will receive power. You will be my witnesses.
Acts 1:8, NCV

Right now we are walking around with dynamite inside of us – the dynamite of God's power, the Holy Spirit. And when we lead worship, the dynamite power of God's Spirit is there to blow apart the prison bars that hold people in, to smash away the chains of fear, and breathe the life of God into every heart and soul turned toward Him in worship.

When a church as a whole devote their heart and soul to worshipping God, His throne is built in their midst – that means His rule, His reign, and His power is established right there, in that congregation of people – when their hearts are turned toward Him. That makes us as a people unstoppable; that makes our congregations unstoppable, because we become carriers of God's presence, like the Ark of God's Covenant that was carried before the children of Israel. Before the Ark even statues of idols fell (1 Samuel 5:3). When we carry God's presence, heaven is able to invade our world – to bring healing, to being peace, to bring comfort, to bring justice and reconciliation.

At Pentecost we remember that God took a bunch of devoted, sold-out, regular, everyday people and changed the world THROUGH them by releasing the power of heaven INTO them. Not even the prospect of death held them back. The Holy Spirit is still on earth, ready to move through a people who are devoted to God.

Unique

God has called you. God has a unique calling for you that only you can walk in, a purpose that only you can fulfill. God has opportunities set up just for you, some because they play a significant part in your life, some just because He wants to bless you. And nothing we have done, are doing, or will do, can change God's heart toward us, because His heart was fixed before He created everything.

Our team has a unique calling and expression, made so because we each bring our uniqueness, our gifting, and our passion to serving our vision of carrying God's people and carrying God's presence. We're not part of a team just to do a job, providing a musical service. God's thoughts go way beyond mere tasks or jobs, but to lives expressing and reflecting His glory, and His life and power and love.

Let's not be defined by the tasks we perform (or wish to perform) but by all that God says we are and has done in us, and then serve His house from that understanding, that knowing of who we are in Him.

What kind of musician/ singer do you want to be?

#singing #musicianship #heart #excellence #great

That's a really important question to ask yourself – what do you really want to do with your singing and/or musicianship? How far do you want to take it?

Before I started learning guitar, way back when, I went to a Baptist church in Devon, and in the evenings their services were a bit more livelier, using more modern songs with a band. The band included two guitarists who both used the same very basic *strum-strum-strummy-strummy* style of playing, and I remember watching them and thinking, "I do not want to be that kind of guitarist – the church deserves better; God deserves better! I can do better!" That observation – which in retrospect I realise was also a little arrogant: I was young! – informed the way I learned, and continue to learn, to play the guitar.

In Psalm 33:3 David writes,

Sing to Him a new song; play skillfully with a shout of joy.

In Chronicles 2:13, Solomon is preparing to build the temple and requests the help of Huram who is 'a skilful man' to oversee the craftsmanship. In Exodus 35 (particularly verse 35), Moses is talking about those being used to build the tent that will be the centre of worship for the nation of Israel, that they are filled with skill to do all manner of work. These verses represent a heart of excellence to do things well for God's house.

It's very easy to settle at a certain level of skill or understanding of musicianship or singing, but is that really the kind of musician or singer you want to be? There are too many average musicians and singers in the worldwide church today, who have decided to settle with where they are, and stick with what they know. Is that what you want to be like? Or do you want to be a great musician or singer? Being great doesn't mean being famous; it just means that your attitude is different to those who have decided to remain average.

A great musician or singer is always learning, stretching themselves a little bit each time, able to take correction, happy to give as much or as little in their playing or singing as is required to serve the moment, not looking for recognition but to serve those they work with and the sound they are all creating.

Ask yourself seriously, what kind of musician/singer do you want to be, and then change whatever needs changing so you start heading in that direction.

Always leading

#carry #leadership #GodsPresence

In two days He will put new life in us; on the third day He will raise us up so that we may live in His presence and know Him.
Hosea 6:2-3, NCV

Four hundred years before the cross, Hosea prophesied this verse, revealing not just that Jesus would die on the cross and be raised to life, but that God intended for it to involve us too. His desire was always that we would have new life, and that that life would be lived in His presence with a greater understanding of Him and all that He is. Right now we are alive in His presence, and we carry His presence into every life situation we experience, good and bad. Our vision is to carry God's presence into the time of corporate worship when we meet together, but that carrying continues after the meeting.

We are all leaders in life because our lives are now given to the cause of God's kingdom, leading the lost to a loving, merciful, healing and welcoming God. It's easy to allow the things of life to weigh us down if all we see are those things of life. God's promise to us is that He has raised us up, given us new life, and brought us into His presence to live and to know Him. The things of life aren't bad, most are actually good and necessary, but let's not let those good things get in the way of the best thing.

Let the things of life take their proper order when we set our heart and eyes back on where we now live and what we now carry – God's presence. We're always leading because we are always carrying God's presence, and He's always directing us towards the people He would have us take His presence to.

*W*orld changers

The teacher sought to find just the right words to express truth clearly.
Ecclesiastes 12:10, NLT

We need to write songs that speak of our church's heart, vision and journey – they are our anthems. We need to be willing to craft our songs – avoid using the excuse "God gave it to me like this" – it's rarely true! The journey of crafting a song enables us to keep our congregations at the forefront of our motivation, and allows God to teach us more. Brian Johnson, worship pastor of Bethel Church wrote on Twitter once, "Songwriters, pray for anthems that rally the church to change the world – God created melody for more than a goose bump. Ask God for phrases He wants in songs, lyrics that say what He is saying, and melodies that drive those lyrics deep[8]."

Our songs can change people's worlds: they can open a window of hope onto desperate and dark situations; they can carry personal words of encouragement from

---

8   https://twitter.com/brianjohnsonM/status/174982730092785664

God to individuals; they can stir up a congregational passion to go. Our songs are not about us, they're about what God can do through His people, and how God's people can become aligned to God's purposes and passion by opening their hearts and engaging with the words and melodies.

I believe God wants to release something fresh and new into our church – all of our congregations – through songs that we have written ourselves. And when I say written I mean crafted, worked on, refined. Songs that we've laboured over to make sure they carry truth and enable our congregations to engage with that truth easily. We are a creative people and the songs are in us, waiting to come out. Like Pastor Andy said on Sunday in church, "Who knows what is waiting to come out of you!"

ision

#vision #hardwork #heart #wilderness #serving

We've said many times how important vision is – without it we will lose life, dry up, and become religious and bound to duty and procedure. Vision takes time to form in our hearts, and it is during the tough times that vision really becomes formed and sharpened in our hearts – if we allow it. When things are hard work, where it would be easy to remain comfortable, or even give up, where going back to how things used to be would actually seem a more sensible option – that's when we need to choose to hold on to our vision and press in to the harvest that God wants to bring to us.

In Hebrews 3:7-8, the writer talks about how the nation of Israel lost sight of why they had to travel through the wilderness (to get to their promised land), and they allowed their hearts to become hardened. We are told: "Today, if you hear His voice [if you catch hold of vision], do not harden your hearts . . . as in the day of trial in the wilderness". Whenever we set our hearts to a vision that God has given us, we WILL go through trial, testing, seasons of wilderness where nothing happens, no growth takes place.

We need those times, because through them God can make the vision stronger in our hearts – as long as we don't allow our hearts to harden. For the Israelites, that decision to forget their vision of heading into their own land was catastrophic, because it meant they never reached the promised land – some even saw it afar off, as they got closer, and yet couldn't enter because they'd harden their hearts.

How tragic, that you can be within touching distance of your vision and yet not enter it because of the state of your heart. You can miss the answers and resources God has brought to you, you can miss new team members, you can miss out on the growth and maturity that God wants to bring in all our lives.

Our vision, in worship team, takes us beyond ourselves and sets our focus on serving our congregations and serving God. The way we do things, the structure we use, the style, the songs, the way we lead and prepare, all flows out of how that vision has impacted our hearts. The trials and tough times will help establish vision in our hearts, so let's never give up or let go.

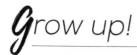

grow up!

#growth #purpose #identity #letgo

Here's a great thought from The Message version of Matthew 5:

> *In a word, what I'm saying is, grow up. You're kingdom subjects. Now live like it. Live out your God-created identity. Live generously and graciously toward others, the way God lives toward you.*
> **Matthew 5:48, The Message**

Are we challenging ourselves to grow up, to leave behind the things that have consumed our lives in the past, or are we just letting life come as it comes, and reacting however we feel like? If we have been unclear as to our God-given purpose, have we done something about it, or are we just carrying on wondering and bouncing from idea to idea? The things that we've worried and fretted about, do they still hold us back? God is daily calling us forward, to grow up, to leave behind the things that are not part of the identity He has given us in Christ. That starts with living selflessly, being givers not takers, goers not sitters.

The days of our lives really are numbered – are we

really going to spend them living in a shallow, self-consumed way or are we going to grow up, lay down our lives for God's kingdom and allow out His kingdom to be revealed through our whole lives. The crux of Pastor Steu's[9] message a few weeks ago in church, on the lepers that Jesus healed, was that God moved in their lives 'as they went' – it didn't happen as they sat around waiting for it, they had to respond to Jesus' word and 'go'.

Let's let go of the things that have hung around our lives, holding us down and causing worry and distraction, grow up, and live out our 'God-given identity'.

---

9   Pastor Steuart Payne is Executive Pastor of Family Church, and the congregational pastor of the Portsmouth congregation.

The little things

It may seem almost picky to keep going on about these housekeeping things, and in the bigger picture they are relatively small things. Like Pastor Andy says, we need to keep the big things BIG and the small things small, which means our primary focus must be on creating an atmosphere of worship and leading the church into it. But it is the small things that make the big things happen well; the small things make the big things happen without any stress or perceived effort. For instance, it's very hard to effectively lead a large congregation like ours in worship if some of the team don't know the songs, or don't know what time they should arrive to set up their stuff, and in not making those small things happen, the big thing gets overlooked or short-changed. Nailing the small things enables the big thing to remain the focus, and allows us to bring all our energy and passion into making the big thing happen.

Song of Solomon 2:15 talks about catching the little foxes that spoil the vine – big foxes aren't that much of a problem: they just nick a few grapes off and run. The little foxes, however, can't reach the grapes so they nibble at the vine itself, and end up killing it. Little things are important to God. But they are just little things. The Vinekeeper's big thing, their main focus, is a nice vintage after all the work of growing, cultivating, reaping, crushing, fermenting and laying down to mature. They'll lose that if they don't deal with the little things, but they can't spend all their time and focus on the little things because they'll forget to actually make the wine.

Let's nail the small things, the principles and ways that we do things, to enable us to step in front of our church and lead them boldly, in peace and in strength, united with the same purpose and desire.

$\int$caffolding or brick?

#building #home #planted

We've just had a great weekend with Stephen Matthew[10], with excellent teaching on building God's House. It's the call for all of us to become builders, and get stuck in. I've often heard from the odd (meant both ways) Christian that they've gone along to such-and-such church "to help them out", or come along to a meeting "to support" the church; that's all nice, but it's not what God has called us to. He hasn't commissioned us to be bits of scaffolding that stand outside of the house and provide support for a period. He's made us as bricks, cemented into the very structure; there through thick and thin, sun and storm. If you took a brick away from the house it was built into, you'd soon notice! Gaps cause weakness, allow rain and wind in, and let warmth out.

Here's a challenging thought: if you stopped doing what you did, would anyone notice, would something seem not right, would things not work so well together? I hope so, for all of us, because even the seemingly

---

10 Stephen Matthew has served as a leader, pastor and teacher – stephenmatthew.com

smallest part played has a massive effect on the overall house. One of my favourite thoughts from FC United was the fact that, when the wall of Jerusalem was being rebuilt in Nehemiah 3, people who's training was in working with gold, or creating incredible perfumes, didn't feel limited by their training but got stuck in with what was needed (can you imagine walking along the finished wall and suddenly stopping because some of the bricks smelt nicer than the last ones, or all of a sudden the wall started sparkling?!); they weren't limited by age or gender, either (hence one section of the wall that was coloured pink and covered in flowers: Nehemiah 3:12 ;)).

They built because it was their home, they were planted there – they weren't just visiting or helping out.

Time to Go

Go through, go through the gates! Make the way ready for the people. Build up, build up the road! Move all the stones off the road. Raise the banner as a sign for the people.
Isaiah 62:10, NCV

This is one of the verses that God gave me when we started as Worship Pastors of Family Church, and it's one of those verses where God reveals more stuff the more you read it. Back then it really seemed to be talking to me about the songs we use, and how they'd direct people to God, but now I can see more of what God is saying through it and it's right for right now! Our Empower Conference is all about "GO!", and comes after Andy's messages last year and the launch of one of our new congregations reflecting our transition into becoming a missionally-motivated church. This verse starts with the command to GO – go, leave the city, get out there, beyond what's safe and what we've come to know. It's a sending out with a purpose, though – to make the road into the city ready to take all the people coming in:

- the road must be made strong and built up;

- the path must be cleared of rubble and obstructions;
- the people must have clear direction as to the way they should go.

This verse speaks to so many areas of the worship team, including the songs that we use and the music we play, as well as our attitude and commitment, our selflessness and boldness.

Go

Let's think outside of ourselves, not looking to what is comfortable for us but to what will help others. The Bible calls us to prefer others above ourselves. That's got to be in our thinking and our actions.

Build

Let's make what we do strong musically, and let's make each other strong by encouraging and supporting each other. Music creates a pathway for people, and so does community.

Clear

Let's not allow anything to be left that could cause anyone to stumble, or to be hurt. When a road gets used a lot, the top layer crumbles and can cause more damage through use – it's part of life. But let's keep all that we do clear from offences, worries or niggles, and when they show, clear them away quickly.

Lead

Give people something to follow, something worth following. People aren't led by great musicianship; they're led by passion. Praise and worship without passion is just religion.

Carrying God's presence

We thoroughly believe in excellence and doing the very best with what you have, and believing for the growth of our resources and skills (and putting in the hard work). Underpinning that, though, is the main thing – to carry, and bring to every area of our lives, the presence of God. The pastors have been preaching these last few weeks about walking in God's favour, and this comes when we allow God's presence to impact to the very core of our being and be poured out into every area of our lives.

When we lead worship as a team, we lead from the presence of God that abides in us – if we just led from our skill or understanding, or from previous experience, we would not be leading from a place that connects the congregation to God's presence, we're just connecting them with our skill and ability. Skill is great but it won't change people's lives, it won't release them from bondage and hurt, it won't open their eyes to truth and overwhelm them with a revelation of grace. We don't do any of that – it's all through God's presence, the abiding anointing and empowering of the Holy Spirit that describes Jesus' ministry in Luke 4 and Acts 10:38.

Our walk with God is what empowers us to serve; and even when our walk seems shallow, God's grace is abundant to us, calling us to make that walk deeper and closer. Let's keep the main thing the main thing, the defining thing in our daily lives.

Revelation

J esus asks the disciples two questions in Luke 9:18-20. The first is "Who do the crowds say I am?", and the second is "Who do you say I am?" Jesus desire in leading the disciples through this kind of questioning was to get them away from the 'going-along-with-the-crowd' mentality to making it personal. Being in a crowd can be great, but a crowd is easily swayed towards the majority, and a crowd's opinions very quickly switch from one way to another. Take the crowd that filled Jerusalem during the week from Jesus' triumphant entry up at the start until He was arrested, put on trial and crucified at the end. The same crowd praised Him and then jeered Him, within the space of a few days. Jesus' second question brought it right home for the disciple, and made it a heart issue for them. In Matthew's record of this conversation (Matthew 16:13-17), after Peter has answered that Jesus is the Christ, Jesus explains that this understanding – this knowing of who Jesus is – has been given to Peter by God the Father.

Worship – real worship – comes from a personal

revelation of who Jesus is. It's easy to get caught up in the crowd of praise, but it's just shallow noise if it isn't coming out of your own revelation of Jesus. I remember the first time worship actually meant something to me because I suddenly understood who Jesus was, and what He'd done for me, even though I'd been raised going to church and hearing the Bible all the time. It's when that moment of revelation hits that you realise how much you want to worship God, and how little you really care about what others think or say.

Psalm 119:18 (NIV) gives us a good prayer, especially when we find ourselves struggling to be inspired in worship: "Open my eyes that I may see wonderful things in Your law". Normally 'law' is dry and boring, but when God opens our eyes we suddenly see Him and understand His truth, and what seemed dry and dull becomes life-giving and inspiring. There is so much of God to know and see – He is inexhaustible and eternal, and every time we look to Him we see something new. Let's bring that personal revelation to the crowd and lead them with worship that has depth and passion.

Turn your eyes

#focus #exchange #worship

Worship goes way beyond the songs we sing and the music we play, we know that. Someone once said that "You become more and more like the thing you worship, the more you worship it". I read a tweet recently that said "You know you've worshipped God when you walk away changed". The old hymn goes:

"Turn your eyes upon Jesus, look full in His wonderful face, then the things of the earth will grow strangely dim in the light of His glory and grace" [11].

There is something about worship, that nothing else can do, that works a change in us whenever we give ourselves over to the doing it wholeheartedly. In exchange for the trust, devotion, honesty and dependence that give to God in worship, He does something in us that makes a little more like Him, that draws out the Spirit-filled, Spirit-led life that was birthed in us when we were saved.

---

11 "Turn your eyes upon Jesus", Helen H. Lemmel. Words: 1922 New Spring; Music: 1922 New Spring

It is that exchange that we are ministers of whenever we stand before our congregations, serving God's people by doing all we can to draw out worship and praise that is heart-felt and faith-filled, and serving God by making a way for Him to move in and amongst His people, to bring healing and peace, salvation and purpose, surrender and change. When we take our eyes off Jesus we start to think that it is us – our skill, our dedication, our time – that has brought these great things. We are His instruments, as long as we keep our eyes turned fully onto Him, and make all that we do our offering of worship. All glory to God, who is able!

lorious God

bar

#GodsPresence #power #glorious #distracted

L ast time I wrote about how worship should change us, when we choose to change what we're looking at. Keeping our eyes fixed on God, and not even the manifestations of His presence and power about us, is key to authenticity in worship. The Israelites were surrounded by manifestations of God's presence when they headed out of Egypt to their promised land: they were led continuously by pillars of cloud and fire – not something you see every day, really – and their food fell to the ground without fail every breakfast, waiting to be collected. And yet, as it says in Psalm 106:20 (NCV), "they exchanged their glorious God for a statue of a bull that eats grass"! In the midst of the miraculous, they forgot where it was all coming from and settled for something that had no power, no glory, no presence and no life! I like the way the New Century Version puts it too, to make the distinction so clear – from a 'glorious God' to a 'statue of a bull'. No matter what the Israelites did to their statue, no matter what skill they employed or carefully-worded praise, or clever rationalisation – it was just a statue and

228

it was no comparison to the glory and magnificence of God.

When we fix our eyes on God, the man-made things around us really do pale in significance, not because they are rubbish or badly made or anything like that, but just simply because God is so glorious, so incredibly magnificent, so awesomely and superlative-exhaustingly great. The Israelites were easily distracted, even when God's presence was so clear and evident, because their hearts were distracted with their own desires and needs. Let's be worshippers whose eyes are fixed on Him, even when His power is evident around us; and let's lead worship that draws people to see Him.

Stretch

#stretching #attitude #improve #choice

$\mathcal{S}$tretching is good. We experience stretching in all kinds of ways, from physical to spiritual. The Wikipedia definition of stretching is: a form of exercise in which a specific skeletal muscle (or muscle group) is deliberately elongated, often by abduction from the torso, in order to improve the muscle's felt elasticity and reaffirm comfortable muscle tone. The result is a feeling of increased muscle control, flexibility and range of motion.[12]

There are some great points to draw out from that definition to help us grow as worship leaders and worshippers. Firstly, stretching is deliberate – it doesn't happen by accident or take us unawares, it's something we initiate ourselves and determine to do, because we sense the need for it. We do it in response to an awareness that we're not quite mobile or awake enough. Secondly, stretching is needed to loosen up and prepare for use – it enables us to make sure we give out of our best, and not just what we can be bothered with or feel like doing; it gets our attitude

---

12 https://en.wikipedia.org/wiki/Stretching, accessed 11th January 2017

focused on what we're going to be doing, and what we're supposed to be doing. Thirdly, stretching is needed to improve – to improve skill, to improve understanding, to improve maturity and character. Finally, if we're not prepared to stretch, then when the big exercise or tasks come, we'll get hurt or broken.

Stretching keeps us looking ahead and not caught in a rut; it's a choice to not sit and let things happen, and end up being unprepared, but to ready ourselves, think ahead, be expectant, anticipate growth and new things. We need to keep stretching ourselves physically and spiritually. Paul says in 1 Corinthians 9:24 that we should "run the race to win", and in 2 Timothy 2:15 to "show ourselves approved" – we should make sure we're always stretching ourselves, never getting comfortable, ready to take up the challenge as it comes.

Hungry?

I saw a great Facebook post from Bill Johnson, the pastor of Bethel Church, recently: he wrote that "The hungry listen to learn; the satisfied listen to critique.[13]" I wonder how hungry we are?

Psalm 63:1, in the Message, says "God – you're my God! I can't get enough of you! I've worked up such hunger and thirst for God, travelling across dry and weary deserts". Proverbs 16:26 says "Appetite is an incentive to work; hunger makes you work all the harder." We should always have a hunger for God, for His presence, and for His word; even when we see God supplying our need, we should keep that hunger in our hearts that caused us to seek Him in the first place. Because, when it comes down to it all, it's the 'seeking God' bit that God is really interested in – not that He doesn't care for us at all, absolutely not. He loves us and has promised to supply all our need and knows so much detail about us that he can count all the hairs on our head. No, it's that we, in our relationship with Him, always make seeking

13 https://www.facebook.com/BillJohnsonMinistries/posts/10150337749668387

Him our highest priority. God's promise to supply our need comes after the call to seek Him.

Our hunger for God infects and motivates our whole life, especially the attitudes that form and shape and direct us. A lack of hunger will cause us to 'not be bothered about our personal practice because, hey, we can do it well enough, that's alright, isn't it'. Hunger, as Bill Johnson stated, keeps us learning, wanting to improve, wanting to go deeper, wanting to discover more – and there is so much more for us to discover. As Pastor Andy says, God hides His gifts from us not because he doesn't want us to have them but because He wants us to go find them – it's the journey of discovery that God loves because He shares it with us.

A little yeast

#religion #relationship #heart #GodsHouse

I hate religion. There, I've said it. Actually, that's not such a shocking thing to say in our church, as it's a pretty strong theme throughout our culture. I was once asked to speak at the Sunderland University Christian Union many years ago, and I opened with that statement, and got the reaction I hoped for (stunned silence!), but it allowed me to speak about the difference between worship based on religion and worship based on relationship.

Religion is the enemy's greatest weapon against an effective church, because it lulls a person or group of people into thinking that what they're doing is right and good, when in fact it is drawing them further and further away from God's heart, and making them feel good about it too! Religion is anything that comes from us relying on our own strength, experience, knowledge or preference, and is justified because in the past it worked and was clearly right and must therefore have been blessed by God so let's keep doing it because we don't want to do anything that displeases God.

Jesus said that religion was like a little yeast that gets worked into the bread dough, and puffs it up when it gets baked – which is awkward when you're trying to make flat bread. In the same way, a little religion puffs up our heads in the success of ministry. God is the God of today and tomorrow, as well as yesterday, and God is the God of new (and different) things, as well as old. Religion will stop us in our tracks as we seek to walk in God's new thing today, and God's newer thing tomorrow. Religion will make us think that we're doing the right thing. Religion will make us think we're doing what God wants, and honouring and obeying His word, and anyone who does different is clearly in disobedience. It's such a subtle thing, but its aim is always to pull our hearts away from God's heart.

Relationship is now, is growing, bears fruit, enjoys intimacy, handles change, brings peace and confidence. David, in Psalm 139, asked God to search his heart and reveal anything that was pulling him away from God. That's a big prayer to make because the results could be quite uncomfortable – but David wanted nothing in the way of his relationship with God. As worship leaders – all of us, standing before our congregations and asking them to follow us in corporate worship – let's make David's prayer our own, so we always bring pure, heart-felt worship to God's House.

Potential

It can be hard sometimes knowing what to write in a short space each week, when there's so much I actually want to say. Where do I start? Where do I stop? It's always been my desire to help release people into their potential, and combine that potential together to make something incredible happen for God's kingdom. Our understanding of our own potential can be so limited, and coloured by the past, but what God has put in each of us is so amazing, and the more we know who we are in Christ, the more we know Him, the more we'll see that potential being used to build God's kingdom.

The thing about potential is that it can be used anywhere and in any way – in Physics, potential energy is not 'actual' energy, but just 'unrealised' energy, and it can be expressed and used in any way possible, good or bad. We all have the potential to use what God has given us well, or to waste it, or to use it selfishly or badly. It's when we grow closer to Jesus that He can speak into our hearts the channels – the ideas and plans and opportunities – out of which that potential can flow and become a life-changing power. And when we allow our potential to become part of a greater outflow of everyone's potential, then cities are changed, laws are rewritten, governments yield to truth and hurting people find healing. Even adding your potential to just one other person makes it ten times more powerful (Deuteronomy 32:30 – read it!). That's why we love team so much.

There is so much potential in our team, it's so great to watch it find a greater release and expression. Keep close to Jesus, let His heart be revealed to us, and in us, so it is His power that breaks the yoke and heals the heart wherever we're called to be.

God is able

That's an easy thing to say, and it's a difficult thing to say – easy because we're a faith-filled, Bible-believing-and-declaring kind-of church that knows the power of declaring God's word and God's promises over our lives regularly and consistently; difficult because we're held to those words when we step into circumstances that cause us to decide whether we actually believe them or not, and are going to stay consistent throughout the time that it seems like those words are not true.

The song *God is able*, from the Hillsong album of the same name, was written just before violent fires and earthquakes hit the oceanic area of the globe, and in an article about the album Reuben Morgan wrote that the song[14] took on a whole new life simply because people chose to sing and declare the words of the song despite the desperate situations many of them were going through. That's when faith becomes the determining factor in our worship life. Take Jehoshaphat, in 2 Chronicles 20 – when the nation of Israel were facing utter defeat by the

---

14 http://www1.cbn.com/music/lessons-in-life%26nbsp%3B%26ndash%3B-god-is-able

masses of the Ammonite, Moabite and Edomite armies, they chose to step out with praise saying, in verse 20, (NCV) "Have faith in the Lord your God and you will stand strong."

We as leaders need to make sure that the words of the songs we sing are faith-filled words, not just poetic or inspirational. When we sing by faith, we bring God's presence through the songs and lead the congregation to sing by faith too.

How are you dressed?

I heard a really good message the other day online from Steven Furtick[15], which I want to summarise here. He mentioned about how he recently went to a wedding and on the way had to stop for petrol. As he was filling the car up he realised he was incredibly over-dressed for being at a petrol station and felt he had to explain to other people, whether they were interested or not, that he didn't normally dress in a suit but he was just on his way to a wedding. The point he drew from that was that he wasn't dressed for where he was at that moment, he was dressed for where he was going, and even if others thought he looked a little weird or odd, it didn't matter because the petrol station was not his destination. He dressed for where he was going, not where he was at.

That got me thinking, as we've talked a lot recently about where we're going as a team, and as a church (and I mean all of our creative teams, not just the Portsmouth worship team) – are you dressed for where we are now, or for where we're going? I don't mean

---

15 https://www.youtube.com/watch?v=pqmahNF4w70

your clothing here, obviously, but how we think, how we live, how we walk out God's calling and live daily for Him. God has spoken things over us a team, and over us individually, but have those words made a difference to the way we live and act and speak and think now? Are we carrying on the way we always did because that's what we know, or has what God has said to us started to change us?

When God speaks something to our hearts, a word of direction, of calling, then not only do we need to take hold of those words by faith and speak them over us, we need to start making changes to how we live and what we do, to take us into God's calling. If God had called you to be a sugar beet farmer while you were a wheat farmer, it'd be all very well saying "Yes, I'm a sugar beet farmer, 'cause God says so!", but if you continued to sow wheat in your fields, you'd still be a wheat farmer, and always would be. God's calling requires us to invest in something new, like Abraham picking up his tents and moving in a new direction. Let's check that we're dressing ourselves for where we're going, not where we've reached so far.

Consumed or Consumer

#consume #attitude #devotion

Pastor Andy's message on Sunday was inspiring and challenging, and leaves us with the thought that although we give our time weekly to serve God's house, are we giving it out of what's easy to give or are we giving it even when it's uncomfortable or awkward. Andy's example of the football fan who turns up to support their team rain or shine, in defeat or victory, local or some other part of the country, shows the capacity that we have to give ourselves to something that has captured our hearts. Compare that to the sofa fan (like me, really!) who'll watch football when it's on TV, and maybe buy the odd football shirt when it's on offer at a sports shop, but will never go out of their way to actually show that support come what may – that kind of fan will consume when it suits them but will never give out; they haven't been consumed by their level of devotion.

Dr Leon van Rooyen[16] preached the week before that the level of love or devotion you have for something

---

16 Dr Leon van Rooyen is a missionary, pastor, teacher, evangelist, church planter, and relief worker throughout the globe; https://www.gmrinc.org/about-dr-leon/dr-leon/

will determine the length of the journey you travel with it; and it also defines your attitude on that journey too. Low devotion will result in a poor and negative attitude, where all you'll see are faults. A high level of devotion will cause you to not let the faults deter you but seek to work out those faults as well as build on the strengths. A high level of devotion will develop maturity and character, low devotion will keep you shallow and flakey.

Let's become more and more consumed with God, and with His house, His people. How can we better serve the people God has called us to? Is there more of our lives we could pour out to see God moving in other's lives? Have we set a level of devotion in our lives toward God that needs to be lifted off so that God can work through us in a greater way?

David's example

David was a man who wholeheartedly gave himself to trusting and knowing God. Throughout his whole life he developed his character to become a great leader. As a child he was patient and humble, knowing his anointing was given and not gained. As a teenager he was faithful and full of faith: he served in the background and was not fazed by the giants he had to overcome. When he faced huge challenges as an adult, he was rooted in faith and in God's strength; he saw every situation as an opportunity to seek God and develop his relationship.

For his commitment to improve and develop his character he was given great influence. "The greater your character the more God will entrust to you. The more God entrusts to you the greater your influence!"

We must remember as musicians and singers, gifted creatively, and positioned for all of the church to see each weekend, that everything we do must come from our relationship with God, through wholehearted trust in what He says, and not on the skills, knowledge or experience we have – every situation, big or small, becomes an opportunity for us to allow God to become strong in us and be strong through us. As a team lets be committed to honour the position/anointing God has given us, as 'stewards' of Family Church worship, by developing our character.

elt it out!

The Message version of the Bible is great for putting verses into very bold, down-to-earth language that hits the mark. Read Psalm 105:2 in any other translation and it's a good verse about telling others of the things that God has done. But here's what it says in the Message:

> *Sing Him songs, belt out hymns, translate His wonders into music!*
> **Psalm 105:2, The Message**

That's a pretty good commissioning statement for a worship team – it sums up what we're called to do and the passion we're to do it with: you can't belt something out quietly or emotionlessly! The second half of that verse especially defines our creative mission – take all that we know of God, all that's been revealed to us, all that we understand, and put it into the sound we create, both vocally and musically, through our writing, through our playing, and through our singing. That has to start from a place of relationship – knowing God, seeking Him, walking daily with Him – we have to have something to be able to translate it into something else. Then comes the development and expression of our creative skills, to be able to take what is stirring in our hearts and put it out there for people to engage with. There's a challenge tied up in that, that we should continually be learning and honing our gifts – so that we're able to express what God is doing on the inside of us. King David used to make new instruments so that he could find ways of expressing that worship, thanks and adoration of the wonders of God.

This isn't something reserved for the 'incredibly gifted' – David didn't put any limitations or qualifications on these verses when he wrote them. They were a challenge and inspiration to the whole nation of Israel, and so also to us.

Motivation

Do you know what motivates you? What was it that originally inspired you to join the worship team? Has that changed since?

What motivates us is a very important thing to think about. Often when we get started in serving in a team we're filled with a sense of purpose and drive to meet a need and serve others. But it's very easy, as the weeks go by, for the things that move you to change – as we become aware of the things we need, we start to feel that if we don't meet them, no one will. Or we get caught in a rut of duty: "This is what I do, it's what I've always done". There are many ways in which our motivation can change, often without us realising.

Let's keep a check on what we are motivated by, and get back to that place where we are inspired to lay down our lives to serve others, where we give all that we can so that other's lives can be changed, healed, restored. Our motivation is key – in Proverbs 4:23 it says that out of our hearts flow the issues of life: in other words, what we're motivated by will influence and affect all that our lives touch. Self-centred motives will never bring life to others, only death. We bring life by laying down our lives, like Jesus did, to serve others.

Do a heart check, and keep those motivations grounded in love, faith and serving others.

lue pegs

#relationship #life

L ast weekend we were up in Suffolk, staying with my wife's parents, and on the Sunday I spoke at their church, which we helped to plant way back in 1995. I 'borrowed' Derek Smith's[17] *Blue Pegs* message and shared about one of my blue pegs that God put in my life literally a week before it completely changed – a friend who'd already been through what I was just about to go through, and who was there in church that weekend.

When we met all those years ago, that blue peg friend got me thinking about learning the guitar properly, and encouraged me in playing at church. At the time, when we met, it seemed quite insignificant, but now, looking back, that meeting pretty much shaped the rest of my life. I even met my wife Ali through him (he's her cousin!). Sharing that blue peg message at my old church reminded me again of how significant the relationships we have right now are, and how much we should protect them from niggles and petty annoyances, because we have no way of

---

17 Derek Smith is senior pastor of King's Church, Bolton, UK; http://kingschurchlife.com

knowing what impact those relationships will have in our future, or what impact we will have on others lives. Proverbs 4:23 tells us to guard our hearts, because out of it flow the issues of life.

Our relationships are stored and nurtured in our hearts, so let's give the same care to guarding our relationships with each other as we would to guarding our own hearts. Then God's life will flow out of all that we do as a team.

No relationship is insignificant.

*E*xperience is key

Experience can make the difference in someone's life. If you have a bad or good experience, you remember it, and it colours your view of that place or event for years to come.

We had an interesting experience with two restaurants today. The first restaurant managed to mess up their service quite badly, so that we ended up being served food that had been handled by another customer, and was not very hot. The waitress then lied to us about the freshness of the replacement food (which was actually just the original food but less warm!). The manager apologised but that was it – no compensation, no courtesy. It was a bad experience. The second restaurant also made an error with our order, and when we pointed it out they apologised and offered us free dessert and coffee – on the whole a good experience. Both could have been bad experiences, but the second restaurant turned it around with their care and generosity.

People's experiences of church can be similar – something bad happens, no one seems to care, people leave and don't go anywhere else; or they find somewhere that makes them feel welcome and part of the family, and they also don't go anywhere else! What we do as part of a church meeting plays a huge part in the overall experience that people – especially new and unchurched people – have when they come to a Family Church congregation, and we must never forget that. We have the opportunity each week to be a part of making a huge difference in the lives of people who need help, who need hope, who need healing, who need friendship.

Our own experience of church is so much better when we help make someone else's experience great.

ulture

#culture #passion #serving #nextgeneration

I did a search on dictionary.com[18] for the meaning of the word 'culture' and got some interesting results back:

- Culture is the quality in a person or society (or team) that arises from a concern for what is regarded as excellent in arts, letters, manners, scholarly pursuits, etc.
- Culture is the behaviours and beliefs characteristic of a particular social, ethnic or age group.
- Culture is the sum total of ways of living built up by a group of human beings and transmitted from one generation to another.

There were a few others related to soil and biology, but those three stood out.

What defines, directs and drives us as a team comes from our concern, or passion, for excellence in what we do; it comes from the combining of all we are passionate about, all that we set as high priority (and also low priority), and all that we enjoy and flourish

---

18 http://www.dictionary.com/browse/culture, accessed 11th January 2017

in. And all of that affects those we serve and those who would aspire to serve with us.

Two things to point out:

1) Let's continue to bring all that we are to the worship team – never treat as 'a job we do on Sundays' but see it as a part of the outflow of God's life through you to the world you have contact with. We are individuals with influence serving together as a team with a much greater influence, and each of us bringing our best enables and releases the whole team to bring our best.

2) Consider that what we do now is not just for now but influences the next generation, and generations to follow. All that we do, on and off the stage, is watched and will be modelled. Let's pass on a great culture.

uilding

#building #responsibility

After we've had such a great Empower[19] weekend, I want to encourage you with a verse from 2 Peter 1:

> *Don't lose a minute in building on what you've been given, complementing your basic faith with good character, spiritual understanding, alert discipline, passionate patience, reverent wonder, warm friendliness and generous love, each dimension fitting into and developing the others.*
> **2 Peter 1:4, The Message**

We need to take all that we've gained over the last week, and even the last few months, and make sure we're building our character, and developing our relationships, and allowing our hearts to be filled with the awe and wonder of knowing Jesus. It's out of this that flows our expression of worship that includes how we serve and our creativity. And the key of this verse is that it is our responsibility to build character, love, patience and all the other things into our love – we can't just sit around expecting God to make it all happen while we do nothing. We need all these things to grow in

---

19 Empower Conference: http://family.church/empower-conference

our lives, because we're not here just doing a job, but living life together, the way God intended.

This list in 2 Peter 1:4 is a great standard to hold over all that each of us do, in our life but particularly in worship team.

Everything we need

#provision #serving #relationship

Last week I looked at some verses in 2 Peter, things we need to take responsibility to add to our lives. A few verses back from that list it says this:

> *Jesus has the power of God, by which He has given us everything we need to live and serve God.*
> **2 Peter 1:3, NCV**

That's a great promise, and one we need to remind ourselves of continually, as all that we do to serve God and His house is through what He has given us, and when it looks like we don't have what it takes, we find that God has given us all that we need.

This promise gives us strength no matter what size our team is, or how many people we lead in worship each week, because wherever we're serving – in a small group or at a big conference, one service a day or three – God has given us all that we need, which is way more than we actually realise or are often able to see with our own eyes.

Just after the verse above it says, "We have these things because we know Him." All that resource, all the wisdom, all that ability and creativity, flows out of our relationship with Jesus – getting to know Him, growing in our understanding of His Word, living it out day by day.

Trust and obey

I'm not quite sure why I started thinking about the hymn *Trust and Obey*, but the other night I couldn't get the lyrics of the chorus out of my head, so I Googled it to find out more. The lyrics are very well known:

> *"Trust and obey, for there's no other way to be happy in Jesus but to trust and obey."* [20]

The story behind this hymn comes from when one of the writers, Daniel Towner, was at an evangelistic meeting held by Dwight Moody, in the 1880's, and heard a new believer stand and say, "I'm not quite sure. But I'm going to trust, and I'm going to obey". He then took that though to his friend John Sammis and together they came up with the hymn that still gets sung all over the world today.

There's such simple and powerful faith in that statement, to realise that there's still so much to understand but what is important is to trust God, and

---

20 "Trust and obey", Daniel Brink Towner, John Henry Sammis, 1887. Public Domain.

to obey – to not sit around waiting for answers but to get out and serve, and keep serving and know that God is higher, and greater, and stronger. To some it may seem a very shallow thought – being happy – but really the writers meant so much more than that, when you read the other lyrics of the song. Real peace is only found in Jesus, and that's the message that we bring to the world around us every day, and it's the message that needs to always come through when we lead worship, beyond the notes we play and the words we sing.

Faith stories

Everyone has a faith story, and regardless of how big or small it may seem in our own eyes, our faith story has the potential to bring hope to many people, some if not most we'll probably never even know about. Ali shared her faith story last Tuesday of our move from Stowmarket, in Suffolk – where she had the security and safety of her home town, her family, her University course, my job, the boys in a good school – up to Sunderland where, up until she made the decision to just trust God and step out, there was no certainty of a place on a University course, a house to live, a job for me or a school for the boys. But when she made that decision to trust God within a fortnight all those things had fallen into place.

Our faith stories are more than 'milestones' along the journey of faith – they become part of how we live out our faith and are heard in the outflow of God's life into the lives of those we minister to and do life with. When we stand on the stage to lead God's people, we're not just singing songs that talk about faith, we're declaring with our lives how God has moved on our behalf – to bring about seemingly impossible change, breakthroughs, miracles, changes of heart, provision, healing, and more – and these songs we're singing sum it all up (well, at least part of it anyway!). The songs we lead take on a new life because they have behind them the life-changing power of God, and we lead with an attitude of "God did it for me, and He'll do it for you too!"

More of our faith stories are still being written now. Whatever we're going through, let's remember Who the author of our story is – and if we're not at the chapter where God makes it happen, then it is still to come. That isn't wishful thinking – that is faith, holding onto the promise of God when what we see suggests another ending.

Our heart

Proverbs 20:5, in The Message, says:

Knowing what is right is like deep water in the heart; a wise person draws from the well within.

It takes a bit of effort to draw out of our heart the wisdom that God has put in there for living, the wisdom of the Holy Spirit as He lives in our lives. So many times through His Word God talks about our hearts, and what He has done in them, most importantly that He has made them His dwelling place. It's easy to live out of what we (think we) know, in our minds, the education and knowledge we've gathered, and although some of that is good, some of it isn't and can actually keep us from enjoying 'knowing what is right' when we draw from God's wisdom.

When we serve in God's house, when we're ministering to His people by leading them in worship and creating for them an atmosphere that allows them to engage with God, we have to be careful not to rely on the shallow knowledge we've gained so far, but be always drawing from the godly wisdom that the Holy Spirit is continually speaking to our hearts – and often that wisdom is contrary to what our 'learned experience' would be telling us! Character is developed when we respond to God's wisdom rather than our own or someone else's.

Let's stir ourselves up to always make the extra effort it takes to not stop at our own wisdom but delve deeper into the wisdom of God that He has put in our hearts through His Spirit in us.

Wholeheartedness

Take a look at the story of Cain and Abel, in Genesis 4:3 (and onwards). They are both farmers, they both bring a portion of their harvest as an offering of worship to God, but there's something about Cain's that causes God to 'disregard' it. In verse 4 it says that Abel brought the firstborn of his 'harvest', whereas in verse 3 it says that Cain just brought some of his harvest. It wasn't so much WHAT they brought, but WHY. Abel brought the very first, before he'd even given thought to his own needs – he put God first, he put significance and value on his offering because in his heart he honoured God before anything else. Whereas it seems that Cain just brought some of his harvest, and that it didn't have the same value or significance to him, it didn't really mean anything to him. Abel was whole-hearted toward God, whereas Cain made a half-hearted effort in his worship.

I'm sure the grain Cain offered was good grain, but God saw what was in his heart, and that was what counted, not the actual thing he gave. Interestingly enough, when he was challenged about it, Cain kicked off and lashed out at his brother, killing him in the process. Half-heartedness will always try to shut down wholeheartedness, rather than change and become wholehearted.

Wholeheartedness demonstrates a complete faith and trust in God. Let's continue to pursue wholeheartedness in our whole lives, and not be intimidated when half-heartedness rears its ugly head and tries to shout us down. Our God is greater and we stand on His truth alone.

Sacrifice!

#sacrifice #heart #GodsHouse

Sacrifice can be a bit of a scary, intense word! Sacrifice is all-inclusive, and pretty final. Samuel says in 1 Samuel 15:22 (NKJV) that "to obey is better than sacrifice", and I used to think that this was a way out of sacrifice, but what Samuel, on behalf of God, is meaning is that the sacrifices were just to sort out the mess afterwards, whereas what God desires is our heart's devotion to him that keeps us away from messing up in the first place. When the Old Testament talks about sacrifice it is referring to ritual, dealing with past committed sins.

In the New Testament sacrifice means something different. Well-known verse Romans 12:1 talks about us being a living sacrifice – but not continually to deal with past committed sin but as a ready and available vessel that is not directed or motivated any more by self. That is something that comes from our heart, not through keeping certain practices or following duty. For us a people who serve God's House week in, week out, sacrifice is us daily laying down our lives so that God's purposes comes first.

We may have great need, we may feel overlooked, we may feel worthy of more praise for what we can do, we may aspire to greater things – but all of that has to be laid on the altar, daily, so that we take part in building continues to be built with God's core values of faith, love and hope – so that Jesus can become greater (in and through us and our church), we must become less.

Leaders at heart

#leadership #heart #GodsHouse #serving #excellence

It is a trap to think, "I'm not a leader, I'm just a humble servant in God's House" – a servant is a leader. But we are neither a servant nor a leader unless it comes from our heart – otherwise it is just religious or spiritual duty, ticking off some boxes.

What God did in our hearts when He made them new is beyond what we realise, but think about it – He gave us a faith that we didn't have before, faith that can move mountains; He gave us a love that is entirely selfless, causing us to become compassionate, forgiving, and willing to give our lives for a purpose that we didn't come up with.

And there's so much more.

As servants who lead and leaders who serve, it is from the rich overflow of what God has done in our heart that we need to keep drawing from and living out of, and not from past experience or what we consider we're capable of or understand. We have excellence because we have an excellent God who has made us excellently and excellence is what is natural to Him and to us.

Let that excellence be the benchmark for what we do, because it'll cause to flow out of us a creativity we hadn't imagined before, or thought possible.

That is worship.

This is who we are

This is a busy weekend, what with FC United[21], a wedding and four services in four locations[22] on Sunday morning.

It's so easy, when it feels like there's lots to do, to allow weariness to guide our thinking and dampen our passion, but it's in those times that we as worship leaders in God's House have the opportunity to take another step up into walking in God's strength and life, and take on the tasks given to us with God-renewed passion and vigour.

Isaiah talks about those who, after waiting on God – not sitting idly around for something to happen, but in a place of readiness and openness to serve – find themselves rising up with God-given strength and power, that causes them to soar above the situations that previously wore them down, and see things from God's perspective.

Paul and Silas found this same strength in the

---

21 FC United is Family Church's bi-monthly all-congregation worship night; http://facebook.com/thisisfamilychurch/events

22 Family Church, as of February 2017, meets in ten locations on a Sunday, including two in the Philippines; http://family.church

Philippian jail, through praise and uninhibited worship. This is a truth and promise for everyone, but we as worship leaders in God's House need to be doing it now so that we can lead the whole church in it.

This is who we are.

God's House

Let's never forget why we do all this – Psalm 69:9 (CEV) sums it all up:

My love for Your house burns in me like a fire.

We are God's house, and it is our love for all that God is, and all the represents Him on the earth – the church – that motivates us and inspires us. More than the joy of singing, more than the pleasure of playing, it's love for God and His people that is the purpose and drive for all we do.

Let's work hard to keep that as our focus, because it is easy to get distracted and make unimportant things become our focus – that is how religion works.

Kingdom leaders

#influence #kingdom #life

Our pastors have been speaking lately about God's kingdom – that we are now citizens of His kingdom, more so than we are of our natural homes of birth. One of the verses that Pastor Andy has spoken from is Matthew 11:12, that describes the attitude of anyone who wants to see the rule, power and flavour of God's kingdom be an influence through their lives – we need to be forceful, to maintain the push, because it is so easy to step back, let things just 'go with the flow', keep it easy. But that leaves us with such a vague, flavourless, wishy-washy expression of all that God is.

There is huge natural and spiritual opposition to God's kingdom, that isn't going to just 'go away' the first time we decide to make a bold expression of our faith. We need to continually stir ourselves up, like Paul encouraged Timothy, to make God's kingdom life our life, and to not accept anything less. When we lead the church, we need to keep that determination in all we do, even in the moments of quiet and intimacy, to keep pursuing Jesus; keeping Him the prize keeps our focus strong and our motivation pure.

A kingdom life is a passionate and determined life, full of righteousness, peace and joy – let's not settle for anything less.

*g*od's delight

P salm 18:19 says this:

He also brought me out into a broad place; He delivered me because He delighted in me.

God is for us so much, more than we really understand or even believe. It is very easy for us, standing in front of the church each week, to slip into taking pleasure and strength from people delighting in what we do – getting those reassuring smiles, handshakes, and compliments can be nice, but we cannot draw our security and assurance from them. I'm not suggesting that the people who give these compliments are being fake, but that we need to draw our reassurance and strength solely from God and what He thinks of us. His opinion is eternal and unchanging, and He has been very clear on the subject – HE LOVES US. He delights in us, and because of that delight He moves on our behalf to bring us into freedom, peace and abundance.

We want to see growth in our team, we want to see new songs, we want to see more influence and opportunity – that's a real "broad place" we see God bringing us into, and all because God delights in us. Let's draw our strength and security from Him, and avoid the trap of pride and self-importance that comes from desiring the delight of people.

Barefoot before God

When both Joshua and Moses experienced one-off powerful meetings with the presence of God – Joshua with the Commander of God's army, and Moses with a bush that looked like it was burning – God told them to take off their shoes as they were standing on holy ground. In many cultures the removing of one's shoes is a sign of respect, and in others it's a sign of submission, whilst in others it's a sign of new carpets. When Moses and Joshua took off their shoes, they showed submission and reverence to God, to His presence and His instruction. They showed humility, putting aside all pride and their sense of importance (Joshua was the leader of Israel). They showed trust – you can run quicker and are more stable with your shoes on.

Our vision is to carry God's presence to His people, and because of the cross and the resurrection, we no longer experience God's presence as a one-off moment, we walk in His presence daily. We should daily be like Joshua and Moses, submitted to God, honouring His presence and His word, trusting Him. And we should especially have that heart attitude when we stand on stage before God's people, because to lead from any other place is to lead from our own strength, and our own purpose and our own sense of self-importance.

Let's walk barefoot before God every day. Let's check our heart attitude and walk in humility, trust, and confidence in God's grace, life and power working through us.

The way God sees it

#GodsPerspective #vision #character #creative

Our vision is to carry God's people into His presence, and carry God's presence to His people, through character and creativity. I've wondered if I should ever try and work out which is more important – character or creativity – but I realised that God doesn't think about the value of things in the same way as we do. We tend to think accordingly: if we only got so much, then which should we focus on getting more of, to be right with God – how should we balance the little we have. But God says, quite often in fact, that He wants us to have more than enough, to be poured over and flooded with His life, so to God I think it's more of a case of 'how much have we got the faith to handle, because there's always more waiting'. Though our character seems under-developed and our creativity pretty minimal, in God's hands it can do more than enough and leave plenty left over – just like the feeding of the five thousand.

Let's keep reminding ourselves to see how God sees, through His word that gives life and turns our value system upside-down.

Confidence

Our confidence is not rooted in what we can do, or what we have done before, but completely in who we are in Christ – we are God's children, we have been completely redeemed, purchased through Jesus' blood only and NOT by any of our attempts at living right. That confidence comes from making good choices, not excuses. I can think back to opportunities I missed out on simply because I made an excuse and pulled out, and I know that I'm where I am now because of good choices I made to just trust God and go with what He'd put on my heart. Leading worship is so much about giving the congregation the confidence to worship.

The most encouraging thing anyone has ever said to me about when I led worship was that I gave him the confidence to worship freely. We do that not just through good preparation, but through being confident ourselves, by always holding to the truth that we ARE loved by God, that we HAVE His grace and empowering to do what we're doing, and that no matter what happens, Jesus is exalted.

We should never be making excuses, just great choices. Those choices lead us into God's blessing and provision – the excuses just keep us looking on at everyone else getting blessed while we miss out. Choose to live confidently, and embrace wholeheartedly the call to serve and build God's house, and make God's name famous.

Consider the cost

In Luke 14:28, Jesus speaks about the wisdom of not just having a plan, but making sure you can pay the cost required to bring that plan to fruition. There is a cost involved, for each of us, to walk in what God has called us to – and it's a different cost for each of us. For us to move forward as a team, we each have to be willing to pay the price that this new season is asking of us. If we see this cost as a penalty, something that infringes on our convenience, then we need to take another look at our vision and get it deeper into our heart and thinking, because when vision has captured your heart you don't mind what the cost is.

David had a huge vision to build a temple for God in Jerusalem – his words were "the house to be built for the Lord must be exceedingly magnificent, famous and glorious throughout all countries" (1 Chronicles 22:5). That is a big vision – imagine building a complex now that had that statement as its design brief! But that is what we're building now, with people and changed lives. If we can see what it is God wants to do through us, then the cost becomes inconsequential – who wouldn't give their lives for something that burnt so strongly in their hearts.

Vision comes with a cost, but if that cost seems too much then we must get back to vision and ask God to burn it deeper in our hearts. Let everything we do flow out of vision.

Zeal

Psalm 69:9 (NIV) says this:

Zeal for your house consumes me.

In the New Century Version that verse reads, "My strong love for your temple completely controls me", and the New King James translates that last part as "has eaten me up". David describes his passion for God and God's House VERY clearly in this verse, and the second half of that verse goes on to describe how he takes insults against God's House personally. David's love for God's House was an extension and an expression of His love for God, that wasn't based on the position to which God has brought him in life (richest in the land, king of all he saw, victorious in every battle) but on his relationship with God, knowing that God always had been, and would always continue to be, for him, even when he made terrible, selfish mistakes or had great successes. That's something that happens at heart level, not emotion/understanding level; and when it does, it consumes us completely and causes us to honour and desire the best for everything that God is and does, which right now is through His people, us, the church: His house.

Just like David, let our deepening relationship with God be expressed through love for His house – His people, and the expression of church to this community and this nation.

Keep dwelling

Keep dwelling on our vision, keep the words turning over in your mind and heart, and let the Holy Spirit speak His purposes for you into your spirit for your life and for your part in this team. These things take time – fruit always takes time to bear – but it is essential we know what God has called us to, and that we devote ourselves to Him, and what He has called us to. God is bringing great influence and opportunity to our church, to every part of it, but it takes character, not talent, to walk in it, and creativity to make the most of it.

Character is a deep-rooted heart thing, and brings an authenticity to what we do. Creativity demonstrates the majesty, vibrancy, diversity and love that God has for His whole creation – why make one butterfly when you can have thousands of varieties (badly clichéd example, I know, but you get my point!). When people come to church for the first time, they need to see both – authenticity in what we do, and a love for unlimited ways in which God can be honoured through our gifts and talents. Let's leave shallow, knowing-the-right-moves living behind for good, and live devoted and passionate about our relationship with God.

Carry God's presence
to His people, and
carry God's people
into His presence,
through character
and creativity

THEME INDEX

ABOUT THE AUTHOR

Matt Lockwood is a child of the 70's, born in Woolwich, London. He started playing guitar in the summer of 1990, and joined his church's worship team later that autumn, playing for morning services, house groups and youth meetings. He has since served as worship leader and worship pastor in small and large churches, as well as speaking and leading at the occasional conference, and coaching other worship team leaders.

He met his wife Ali in 1992, and they were married in 1995. They have three children – Zach, Caleb and Matilda, and live in a small seaside town on the South Coast of England. Matt juggles being a house husband (Ali is a primary school Headteacher), graphic designer, publisher and worship pastor of Family Church, a multi-congregation church based in Portsmouth, UK.

He loves reading, cooking, Star Wars, The Office (US), Owl City, Michael W Smith, and his family. His worst mistake was blending the words 'crowned' and 'wrapped' whilst leading worship. #awkward.

PRAYER

We hope you have enjoyed this book and that is has been both a blessing and a challenge to your life and walk with God. Maybe you just got hold of it and are looking through before starting. If you have never asked Jesus into your life and would like to do that now, it's so easy. Just pray this simple prayer:

Dear Lord Jesus, thank You for dying on the cross for me. I believe that You gave Your life so that I could have life. When You died on the cross, You died as an innocent man who had done nothing wrong. You were paying for my sins and the debt I could never pay. I believe in You, Jesus, and receive the brand new life and fresh start that the Bible promises that I can have. Thank You for my sins forgiven, for the righteousness that comes to me as a gift from You, for hope and love beyond what I have known and the assurance of eternal life that is now mine. Amen.

Good next moves are to get yourself a Bible that is easy to understand and begin to read. Maybe start in the Gospel of John so you can discover all about Jesus for yourself. Start to pray – prayer is simply talking to

God – and, finally, find a church that's alive and get your life planted in it. These simple ingredients will cause your relationship with God to grow.

Why not email us and let us know if you did that so we can rejoice with you?

The Great Big Life Publishing team
info@greatbiglifepublishing.com